"If we're going to fix the biggest problems we have in the world today, there's no way around it: we're going to need to work together. Ultimately, this is not just a book that every leader should read. It's a message the world itself needs right now."

—Adam Braun,
founder of Pencils of Promise and MissionU

DREAM TEAMS

WITHDRAWN

DREAM TEAMS

Working Together Without Falling Apart

SHANE SNOW

WITHDRAWN

PORTFOLIO / PENGUIN

Portfolio/Penguin
An imprint of Penguin Random House LLC
375 Hudson Street
New York, New York 10014

Most Portfolio books are available at a discount when purchased in quantity for sales promotions or corporate use. Special editions, which include personalized covers, excerpts, and corporate imprints, can be created when purchased in large quantities. For more information, please call (212) 572-2232 or e-mail specialmarkets@penguinrandomhouse.com. Your local bookstore can also assist with discounted bulk purchases using the Penguin Random House corporate Business-to-Business program. For assistance in locating a participating retailer, e-mail B2B@penguinrandomhouse.com.

Library of Congress Cataloging-in-Publication Data

Names: Snow, Shane, author.
Title: Dream teams : working together without falling apart / Shane Snow.
Description: New York : Portfolio/Penguin, [2018] | Includes index.
Identifiers: LCCN 2018014633| ISBN 9780735217799 (hardcover) |
ISBN 9780735217805 (epub)
Subjects: LCSH: Cooperativeness. | Small groups—Psychological aspects. |
Teams in the workplace. | Interpersonal relations. | Interpersonal conflict.
Classification: LCC HM716 .S58 2018 | DDC 658.4/022—dc23 LC record available at
https://lccn.loc.gov/2018014633

Printed in the United States of America
1 3 5 7 9 10 8 6 4 2

Book design by Laura K. Corless

CONTENTS

———⊕⊕———

DREAM
TEAMS

FOREWORD

—⚭—

by Aaron Walton, activist, model,
and founding partner of Walton Isaacson

When I was in third and fourth grade, my grandfather used to ask me, "What will you do today to make the world a better place?" Every morning when I saw him, I knew that's what he was going to ask me.

Growing up as a gay black kid in Massachusetts in the 1960s and '70s was not the easiest. I was in Roxbury, a rough part of Boston.

But every single time I saw him, Pops asked me the exact same thing.

Not: "What will you do today to make your life better?"

But: "What will you do today to make the world better?"

And I've got to tell you, I remember thinking, "That's part of my job."

On my journey, I became very aware of the massive power that working as a team has to make something bigger and better than just myself. Because of how I grew up, I have always felt the need to be a leader and to help move things along, but I also realized that progress is not a solo journey.

That philosophy has been how I've approached everything.

For example, when I started my latest company, my partner Cory and I sat down with an ambitious mission: "What if we wanted to create the planet's most interesting agency?" we said.

When we sat down and mapped it out, the first thing that we worked on was not what clients we would go after, or what creative work we would do. Those are the typical things agencies start with.

Instead, the question we asked ourselves was, "What team of people will be able to reach this vision?"

We decided that if we got the right kinds of different people in the room—and we tapped into their unique points of view—that would be what got us there.

We believed that ideas could be pushed forward in a more productive and innovative way if you have a team of people with diverse backgrounds. And not just culturally diverse, but also by discipline. I knew the research that shows that teams like these can be more successful because different people have to work harder to get their points across. When we're with people who aren't like us, we have to marshal more resources, brainpower, to help convince other people of why a different direction might be the right direction. And this helps us break through.

Over the years, we put this into practice. And we've built a team that is truly different, and truly does some of the planet's most interesting work, furthering social causes while building businesses at the same time. When we pitched and won a Super Bowl campaign, for example, we weren't successful just because of the idea. When we made a viral video showcasing Hispanic Americans taking pride in their work and heritage, it didn't go viral just because of the concept itself. There are a billion great ideas. It was how our team worked together that made these things happen. It was about how we brought that great idea to life by tapping into the zeitgeist of the people in our group.

Real innovation comes from our differences. Ideas get better when we challenge each other.

But here's the thing.

It's not comfortable. It's messy. It's like a Pollock painting—it looks like chaos. As humans, we want to avoid conflict. The tension points between us makes us better. But getting it to work right is hard.

That's why I'm excited about this book.

I think we're much stronger collectively than we are individually. If you think about every great breakthrough in the world, it's genuinely linked to when people have been working as a team, when we have been thinking about, "What can we do that's going to make life better for someone else?"

Am I naive to think that that's the way the world should work?

We're all trying to get to our mountaintop. And once we get to it, we're looking for another mountain to climb. To make that journey, we need each other.

The answer to my grandfather's question will be different every day for each of us. The fact that we will need to do it together will not.

And when we win, we'll all win.

ACKNOWLEDGMENTS

This book is a product of myriad collaborations itself. There are too many people to thank for making it happen.

But here are a few:

Frank Morgan, Esq.
Jim and Merry and Ryan
Tamsyn and Karina
Eric, Jenn, Allie
Dan S.
Aaron, Erin
Nicole, Eli
Jess, of course
Joe and Brandon and Brian and Masha
Nir, Maria, James, Steve, Mark, and the gang
Adam, Jon, Brad, Paula, James
My sensitivity readers: Grace, Zainab, Ebony
My fact-checker, Cara, and copyeditor, Tricia
David, God rest

And many more . . .

DREAM TEAMS

"I just let them do what they wanted to do."

At the height of the Cold War, the Soviet Union and the collective nations known as the West competed over practically everything. Politics. Technology. Chess. Math. Going to space. But there was one arena in which there was no competition.

Hockey. The Soviets owned that one.

Between 1960 and 1990, the Soviet national hockey team won nearly every international match it played, and that's the dullest way to put it. The Russians *destroyed*.

In the 1976 Olympics, for example, they trounced the United States 6–2, mopped up Finland 7–2, and beat Czechoslovakia in the finals for the Olympic gold medal.

Their *fourth* gold medal in a row.

The Soviet coach was a freak, a legend, a Zen master on ice. Anatoly Tarasov was his name. He made his young athletes study chess and dancing. They practiced jumping off walls. They learned to do ninja moves wearing skates. They sang songs with lyrics like "cowards don't play hockey." Tarasov's mash-ups of athletic and mental conditioning made his students see the world—the whole world—as relevant to hockey.

Another freaky coach followed: Viktor Tikhonov, a Soviet army general who was known for his dictatorial style, ruthless eleven-month-long practice regimens, and the hatred his players had for him.

Out of this ice-dojo arose a group of athletes that would go down in history as not just one of the world's best hockey teams, but one of the best *sports* teams of all time. They were called the Red Army. Here was their most famous starting lineup, known as the Russian Five:

Viacheslav "Slava" Fetisov, defenseman. Natural-born leader and decorated hockey god. Both charming and terrifying, "like a bear." Said to be one of the greatest players ever.

Alexei Kasatonov, defenseman. Disciplined, patriotic, and unflinching. Fetisov's best friend on and off the ice.

Vladimir Krutov, forward. Known as the "Russian tank." Standing five feet nine and weighing close to two hundred pounds, Krutov was a beer keg on skates and the reliable "soul" of the team.

Igor Larionov, center. Called "The Professor," Larionov was cerebral, a tactician. Skinny and deceptively tough, his specialty was misleading opposing players.

Sergei Makarov, forward. Makarov was a sniper, feared by goalies everywhere. He could find the back of the net from anywhere on the rink.

They were backed up at the net by legendary goaltender Vladislav Tretiak, known for his stoicism and quick thinking. And this doesn't include the dozen other talented players in the club at a given time, each with his own fearsome quirks and specialties, such as longtime team captain Valery Vasiliev, who was known for punishing opponents while hungover from partying all night and even once finishing a game after having a *heart attack* on the rink.

You get the idea. They were monsters.

But it wasn't just a stack of great individual players that made the Soviet team dominate. North American teams were known to scout young hockey players from junior leagues and groom them for the pros from absurdly young ages. Canadian pro hockey players tended to be flawless skaters with big muscles.* During much of the Red Army's winning streak, Canada actually had players with better individual statistics on its national team, such as the legendary Wayne Gretzky.†

No. It was their style, the Russians insisted, that made their team special. No matter who was on the ice, opponents claimed the Red Army could read minds. It could be Fetisov and Kasatonov defending the net as one. Or champion center Sergei Fedorov circling the defense, distracting them while a teammate sliced in for a shot. Or, in later years, it could be Vladimir "The Impaler" Konstantinov gliding through the enemy like a human spear, passing the puck between the opponent's legs. Regardless of the configuration, they were unstoppable.

After losing the Canada Cup to them, Wayne Gretzky would tell *Sports Illustrated* that the Russians simply "dismantled" him. US

---

*And big mullets.

†It's worth mentioning that it wasn't until 1988 that the Olympic Games started allowing "pro" players who made full-time salaries in sports like hockey and basketball to play. So up until then, the Soviet players, who lived under communism and got around the "pro" rule, ended up playing against amateurs in the Olympics. Until then, it was only all the other international tournaments that Canada and the USA got to send their best players to the Soviet slaughter.

coaches would describe the Red Army as having "a sixth sense" and
"eyes in the back of their head." While Western hockey teams played
aggressively—smashing into opponents like it was rugby—the Soviets performed a deadly ballet. They took a sport synonymous with
beer and brawling and turned it into an art form.

Here I have to pause. I have a confession to make:

I'm not really into sports.

Forgive me, Red Sox Nation. Put down your pitchforks, Cheese-
heads. You can blame my dad. He was an engineer working in
the sports-starved desert of southeast Idaho. I grew up thinking
a wide receiver was something you plug into a radio. In my home,
The Game was never "on." To this day I rarely tune in to televised
sports. Also:

The old Soviet national hockey team footage is *mesmerizing.*

Watching them play—sports fan or no—you just can't look
away. They were so good that when Team USA narrowly beat them
at the 1980 Olympics, the moment was declared a "Miracle on Ice."[*]

It turns out that "Political Skulduggery on Ice" would have been
a more accurate description. While the win was certainly cathartic
for America, the Russians essentially blew the game because of politics. USA's deciding goals happened after Coach Tikhonov pulled
three Red Army players out of the game, including goaltender Tretiak, and replaced them with players from a KGB-sponsored hockey
club in an attempt to score points with the Kremlin. And *still* the
Soviets nearly won.

Galvanized by that defeat and vowing never to divide their team
again, the Red Army reigned for the next ten years. They won the
gold in 1984 and 1988. They placed first in just about every other
international championship, winning hundreds of games by embar-

---

[*] Starring Karl Malden, in a 1981 movie of the same title.

rassing margins. The crew would go back-to-back years without losing a single match.

And then the Cold War ended. The Iron Curtain fell. For years the Soviet players had been paid peanuts, but now they were free to play for Western teams with real salaries. One by one, the stars of the Soviet national team left Russia to play for their former enemy: North America's very own National Hockey League.

Fetisov and Kasatonov went to the Devils. Krutov and Larionov went to the Canucks. Makarov went to the Flames. Each was heralded as a hero that would change the franchise.

And each sucked.

None of the Russian Five's new teams won championships. Their stats tumbled. Many of the great Red Army players were older now—almost washed-up. They didn't have the same chemistry with their new US and Canadian teammates—nothing like back home. Even when they ended up on teams stacked with hotshots, somehow they couldn't seem to win. And on the rare occasion they got teamed up with a fellow player from the old days, it made little difference: they still couldn't bring back that old magic. Tarasov's choreography and Tikhonov's discipline were no match for the ever larger and fiercer North American players. The Russians could adapt, but they couldn't compete like they used to.

Team owners lost patience. Kasatonov got traded to the Blues, then the Ducks, then the Bruins. Makarov was traded to the Sharks. Fetisov went into a slump. In the old Soviet days he was one of the top scorers in the world, but in New Jersey he wasn't even near the top of his own team. Sports headlines, once jubilant about the Red Army coming to America, now sounded the alarm. "Devils Hit a Drought in Scoring," the *New York Times* lamented in 1992, noting that some saw a lack of teamwork at the root of the problem.

Those magic years as impossible champions lasted longer than Fetisov or any of his comrades would have dreamed when they started out as kids. But like most such stories, the magic finally fizzled out.

When Ronald Reagan referred to the Soviets as "monsters" during the run-up to the 1980 presidential election, he wasn't talking about their hockey players. He was talking about the Soviet Union as a whole, as enemies whom the United States would make sure were "destroyed with nuclear weapons" if it came to it.

Soviet premier Nikita Khrushchev wasn't talking about hockey either when he famously told Western diplomats, "We will bury you." For decades, those words reverberated across the Northern Hemisphere.

So while Tarasov's budding young stars sang songs about hockey together, their peers in public schools sang about how to duck and cover under a desk if and when The Bomb went off. When they traveled to America to slap around little rubber disks into little nets for crowds of beer guzzlers, their countries were busily manufacturing weapons of mass destruction. Though all those kids really wanted to do was play, hockey—like chess and space and all the other competitions—became a proxy fight for two countries who hated each other and their ideas: a fight that by all accounts could escalate to nuclear war and the end of civilization.

Ironically, to develop the nuclear technology that their countries threatened each other with in the first place, scientists from Russia *and* America had to get along—and collaborate with women and men from Germany and France and Poland and Britain, and many other places. They built on each other's work, shared research and laboratories, and discovered how smashing atoms together created heat, which could make steam to turn turbines, which could make electricity.

I was keen on this story growing up, because that engineering job my dad worked at in the Idaho desert happened to be a nuclear power plant. This is how the seed of science was planted in my little nerdy heart, leading me to pursue my career in science and technology journalism. I learned from a young age how the brilliant work of chemists and physicists and electric engineers and tinkerers of all kinds led us to figure out how to smash atoms together and harness the resulting heat to make electricity. And I learned that this was how every other breakthrough in history happened, from the steam engine to stuffed-crust pizza: when humans put their heads together.

Physically speaking, we are built for collaboration. Our brains are equipped for empathy. Our tongue and larynx can produce a range of sounds that put a dolphin to shame. The whites of our eyes are three times larger than those of other primates, helping us track what the other is looking at when words aren't possible. These features of body and brain raised us from a humble subtropical survivor to the global apex predator that built the pyramids, painted the Sistine Chapel, and filmed season 8 of *Real Housewives of New Jersey*.

And yet, as the Cold War and every other reminiscent conflict between humans remind us, there's a depressing side to our nature when we come together. Our brains are wired to collaborate but also to be suspicious of other tribes—to "bury" those who don't look or think like us. And statistics show that working together is bound to be frustrating even when we start off liking each other.* As one famed organizational psychologist puts it, "Virtually all of the studies unambiguously reveal that individuals outperform teams in terms

---

*I became viscerally aware of this when running the media technology company two partners and I launched in 2010, called Contently. We helped pioneer an industry and give thousands of people jobs because of the way we worked together. But though we'd go on to win awards from Crains and Ad Age for being one of the country's "Best Places To Work," our biggest challenges through the years almost always boiled down to the same thing: people, working together.

of both quantity and quality." We pull a little less hard on the tug-of-war rope when we're part of a crew than when we're by ourselves. We shout only 74 percent as loud in a group of six as we do alone, even when we think we're shouting our loudest. And we have repeatedly demonstrated that when we put people together to brainstorm, most groups will come up with fewer creative ideas—and fewer good ones—than the individual members of the group when they were allowed to brainstorm on their own.*

But the hard things in work and life often *can't* be done alone. We know that, too. It takes two people to make a baby. It takes a dozen to make a pro hockey team. It takes the work of hundreds to develop a scientific breakthrough like nuclear power, and thousands to operate a Fortune 500 company. It takes a gosh-darn *village* to raise a child. Major progress requires major numbers of people working together.

When we put our heads together, we hope we'll become better, not just bigger. But the reality is, we almost always *don't*. We have to fight against the inherent drag that comes with group work. And we end up fighting each other. Farm becomes fief. Polity becomes caste. We beat our plowshares into swords† and turn nuclear energy into a bomb. And so, Team USSR and Team USA played hockey in the shadow of two giants with intercontinental ballistic missiles pointed at each other.

Humans need to work together to accomplish anything big. But—in our teams, our nations, our companies and families—our

---

* "Business people," famed psychologist Adrian Furnham of University College London once said, "must be insane to use brainstorming groups."

† Joel 3:10, KJV. Also Don Henley.

collaborative efforts seem to move with all the thrilling speed of a glacier, and often end in an avalanche of our own creation.

And yet! Occasionally we experience an opposite phenomenon.

Every once in a while, we encounter—or sometimes are lucky enough to be part of—a magical moment when a group of people somehow becomes more than the sum of its parts. This is how breakthrough progress happens, from having a baby to harnessing the atom. On those rare occasions it happens to us, we feel limitless.

Like the Soviet National Hockey Team felt during that brief and beautiful stretch of history before it all fell apart.

In 1994, after the hockey players from the Soviet national team had aged over the hill or fallen out of the spotlight in the NHL, Scotty Bowman, the head coach of the Detroit Red Wings, began quietly gathering up the old Soviet national team players to his club.

He recruited Fetisov, who was pushing Old Man Status in sports terms at that point. He got Larionov in 1995. He picked up the young Soviet forward Vyacheslav Kozlov, and snatched up comrade Konstantinov ("The Impaler"), along with Fedorov, whom the Red Wings had drafted a few years before.

And rather than forcing a playbook on them, he stepped back. "I just let them do what they wanted to do," he said.

In their first year, this reborn Russian Five won more games than any other team in the NHL. Larionov went from scoring two points the season before with the San Jose Sharks to seventy-one for the Red Wings. Fetisov tripled his total as well. Fedorov won a trophy.

Suddenly they were unstoppable again.

The following year the Red Wings won the Stanley Cup. And they won it again the next year.

When documentarians asked Fetisov to describe what happened, he said, "Together again on the same team, it was like a fish put back in the water."

This is a book about Dream Teams, about groups of people that make breakthroughs together. Like Fetisov and his fellow hockey players, they do the incredible against all probability. In the chapters ahead, we're going to meet one Dream Team after another: creative agencies, rap groups, software companies, urban planners, social movements, and ragtag armies that pulled off amazing things together. We're going to uncover the secrets of individuals who make outstanding collaborators, and look at what separates groups that simply get by together from groups that get better. And in examining the hidden psychology of great teams, I will argue that there's something wrong with the common wisdom about human collaboration—and a way for us to harness our collective potential better than before.

Our greatest moments in history—not just in sports, but in business and art and science and society—happened when humans defied the odds by coming together and becoming more than the sum of their parts. When they linked arms, stood on the metaphorical shoulders of the giants who came before them, and saw further together.

Those old Soviet hockey players were that rare kind of team that turns the depressing truth about human chemistry on its head. Though they were each excellent players, the synergy that made them the best even after years apart—and with a new American coach—is not explained by skill or talent or practice time. Opposing teams had better player statistics.* Other hockey players had practiced together as many years as the Russians had. But somehow, what Tarasov's kids had between them was special.

There's science behind this kind of magic. Dream Teams are not just random. They're the result of subtle interactions, and ones that are not obvious. In recent years, we've made new discoveries in psychology and neuroscience that can help us unlock the magic that vaulted the Russian Five to greatness. And that science can help us work better together in any field.

So what *is* that special sauce? What are those eleven secret herbs and spices that make some people more amazing together than apart? And conversely, what makes the teams of the most skilled and talented people on paper so often fail to exceed the sum of their parts in real life? What makes our society, full of brilliant and hardworking and passionate people, so capable of destroying itself, when we have more resources and knowledge and technology and beauty between us than ever before?

As we'll discover in the coming pages, the answers are often counterintuitive. The kinds of teams that change the course of history—that transform industries, break cycles of oppression or stagnation, or win hockey championships for decades in a row—are not the usual suspects. What makes them different lies beneath the surface.

But once we understand how it works, the science of Dream

---

* Statisticians who study team sports data at a granular level find that the proportion of "elite athletes" on a team has little to do with whether a team wins championships. Having a superstar tends to help a team score points, but having a lot of superstars does not help a team win. In fact, teams with the best individual statistics tend to lose a lot to teams with lower numbers of stars. Once you get to a certain level of skill—say, professional NHL status—the thing that makes the biggest difference is not how good the players are, but how they work together.

Teams is something that we can apply to everything. From our personal relationships, to our everyday work, to our businesses and causes, to our communities, and to a world itself that desperately needs us to stop breaking down because of each other, and start breaking through together.

This book is about how that magic happens.

ONE

———— ✺ ————

BUDDY COPS
AND MOUNTAINTOPS

"I think I ruined the wedding."

1.

The Chicago detectives were in Baltimore, of all places, investigating a train robbery (of all things!) when they learned about the plot to kill their hometown congressman.

It was February and cold outside the office bearing the name "John H. Hutchinson, Stock Broker" on South Street near Baltimore's Inner Harbor. The office was a front—a temporary headquarters for agents of Hutchinson's private detective firm. The firm specialized in fraud and corporate espionage, particularly for clients who wanted to keep things quiet.

Hutchinson's detectives had inhabited this secret office for several weeks now. They were there at the behest of the president of a local railroad company, a man named Samuel Felton. He'd hired them to look into a rumor about a plot to ruin him by disrupting millions of dollars of train cargo. Local politics were tense in Baltimore at the time, and Felton had feared "an extensive and organized conspiracy" that included members of the city police, or even higher up. Paranoid as he was, Felton decided to hire outsiders to suss out whether the rumors had merit, before involving authorities.

And when it came to that sort of thing, Hutchinson was the best. A classic entrepreneur, he was a school dropout with a knack for solving puzzles. This led him to become a police detective, then to open a private firm. After ten years in operation, Hutchinson still personally masterminded most high-profile jobs.

For the Baltimore Railroad case, he had also staffed his finest crew:

Detective Webster was the principal investigator on the case. He was a tall British immigrant, with curly hair and a beard that can be best described as "hipster."* Webster was tough and experienced and unafraid to kick down a door or jump from a moving train—as he once did while chasing a fleeing suspect. A family man with four kids, he'd earned his stripes as an NYPD officer for over a decade.

Webster's counterpart, Detective Warne, on the other hand, was sly, charismatic, and twenty-eight years old. Where Webster was a decisive man of action, Warne was the agency's smooth talker and master of disguise—thin and chameleonlike, with a knack for getting people to cough up information.

The two had been chasing down Felton's railroad conspiracy at various Baltimore PD haunts for a month when they overheard a rumor that sent them racing back to base. In the course of that month, they had determined that a group of corrupt officials and politically disenfranchised socialites indeed had it out for Felton. But as far as they could tell, the group had done little but talk trash about him and other high-profile figures in Baltimore.

Webster, who knew how to relate to police officers, had been

---

*I'm told that anyone who puts "hipster" in quotes is officially no longer hip themselves. Crap.

buddying up with off-duty drunks at local cop bars. Meanwhile, Warne was spending evenings in disguise at elite social hangouts, eavesdropping on the conversations of potential conspirators. In this manner, the two pieced together the troubling details of what was really afoot:

Basically, it was terrorism. The group, frustrated at the state of national politics that they felt was leaving Baltimore behind, wanted to send a message: the government had failed. "Look at our city," one conspirator confided, "and tell me if we are not going to ruin." They'd considered several ways to draw attention to this point, like ruining Felton's railroad line. But the group had recently cooked up plans to do something much less subtle: assassinate a high-profile congressman who would soon be passing through town.

The congressman—a popular but polarizing Republican—was the perfect target. He represented everything these extremists hated about the current state of politics. They suspected that his death, while shocking, would spark the dialogue they desired. They'd then knock off Maryland's governor for good measure. Each would die as an example, one conspirator said, of a "traitor to God and this country."

The conspiracy reached high. A police captain named Ferrandini had vowed that the out-of-state congressman would "die in this city." And police chief George Kane, who was sympathetic to the extremists' cause, was willing to turn a blind eye.

The congressman had made public plans to travel among the citizens—by train—from Illinois to Washington, with a series of speaking events scheduled en route. After stopping at Columbus, Pittsburgh, New York, Philadelphia, and Harrisburg, he would board a train to Baltimore. There a driver would take him to the Eutaw House, where he would deliver a short speech. After the speech, the driver would take him to a train station a mile away, for a final leg to Washington, DC.

Although it's customary in America for local police to provide an armed escort for visiting politicians—often a showy spectacle of blocked roads and sirens—the plan was for Chief Kane to claim at the last minute that he could not spare any officers to meet the congressman's entourage at the train station. The man and his personal detail would be on their own.

The conspirators would post agents along the route, sending word of the congressman's progress toward Baltimore. They had choreographed a "street fight" to break out as he passed through the vestibule at the train station to meet his driver. The fight would distract the transit security. Simultaneously, a mob of faux commuters would swarm the area. Several of these would be armed men—including at least one police officer—who would proceed to gun down the congressman and his entourage.

When he reviewed Webster's and Warne's intel, Hutchinson spiraled into anxiety. This was much bigger than railroad sabotage indeed. They needed to alert some proper authorities. But how far up did the conspiracy go? Hutchinson dispatched Warne to alert the congressman and advise he go straight to Washington and skip the speaking tour.

But the congressman deliberated: Given the current climate, canceling all these speeches could be politically disastrous. And tipping off the terrorists now would make them harder to catch later. Still, evidence of the murder plot was compelling. He asked Warne: Could they discreetly get him to DC after his final event in Harrisburg—and leave authorities out of it?

Hutchinson reluctantly agreed, understanding that any leak could hamper an investigation into the wider conspiracy. But he was nervous. This was not corporate espionage. It was life and death. And anyone could be a conspirator.

Except for Mr. Felton, Hutchinson decided. He'd enlisted them to investigate these corrupt officials in the first place. He had to be clean. Now it was their turn to enlist him.

So, with Felton's help, the detectives devised a plan.

On the night of the planned murder, after a packed speaking event in Harrisburg, the Republican from Illinois's Seventh District excused himself to his hotel room. He donned the disguise that Warne had prepared for him—a felt hat and slouchy overcoat—and exited the hotel alone through a back entrance. Hutchinson and a bodyguard met him there and accompanied him to the midnight train to Philly. Warne was waiting, having reserved a car for their "family," whose "invalid brother" needed special assistance.

While changing trains in Philadelphia, the disguised congressman stumbled through the station, playing the part of the disabled brother marvelously. The conspirators who camped out to alert the gang ahead didn't notice as the group crossed the station and boarded the next train to Baltimore.

Meanwhile, behind the scenes, Hutchinson's crew were busy altering train routes. They'd secretly arranged for the earlier train to Baltimore to travel slower, and along a side track. This allowed the congressman's train to accelerate and arrive in Baltimore well ahead of schedule.

They arrived early, as planned. Again, no one noticed the "invalid" in the cowboy hat as he transferred with his "family"—to an early train to DC.

Captain Ferrandini and his assassination gang were still waiting outside the Baltimore station as the train left for Washington. The disguised congressman passed through right under their noses.

Detective Warne stayed awake all night as the train clattered past Fort Meade, Glendale, and Landover Hills. The congressman snoozed as his car crossed the Anacostia River and pulled into the station. Then he woke up and stepped out into the drizzly DC morning.

Where he, Abraham Lincoln, was inaugurated the sixteenth president of the United States.

2.

We're going to start our adventure in the science of breakthrough teamwork with cops—small partnerships that have to solve big problems. Because what makes good police work work illustrates the foundational principle upon which Dream Teams operate. This will prepare us to explore all sorts of other kinds of teams, from bands to businesses to armies to social movements.

The foiling of the "Baltimore Plot" to assassinate Lincoln is an excellent case study for us to begin with: We had two groups of collaborators. One was outnumbered, outgunned, and out of time. The other was large, connected, and coordinated. Beating the odds required Hutchinson, Felton, Warne, and Webster to conduct a last-minute symphony, solving a series of problems in a variety of clever ways. They wore disguises, ferreted out the enemy's plans, and orchestrated delicate logistics to save a life—and potentially a nation. And they had to do it all in secret.

In fact, even the name John H. Hutchinson itself was an alias. His real name is one you may have heard: Allan Pinkerton. After the Baltimore Plot, Pinkerton's National Detective Agency became one of the most famous in history.

Which reminds me, there's something else that I need to tell you.

There's something about that charismatic, disguise-loving, twenty-eight-year-old whose work was instrumental to saving Lincoln's life that's germane to our exploration of breakthrough collaboration. It's something that will help us understand the first and most fundamental component of Dream Teams.

It's that if you're like most people, you probably thought Detective Warne was a man.

But she wasn't.

3.

Let us face reality. If the credibility of the FBI is to be maintained in the eyes of the public, the lawbreaker, fugitive, deserter, et cetera, and if we are to continue to be a flexible, mobile, ready-for-anything force of Special Agents, we must continue to limit the position to males.

—J. EDGAR HOOVER (MARCH 11, 1971)

4.

Kate Warne was the first female detective we know about in US history. But it took a long time for there to be many more.

Women weren't allowed to join police departments until thirty years after the Baltimore Plot. It wasn't until even later that police departments assigned any women to be detectives. And the FBI didn't hire a single female agent until 1972.

The ranks of women law enforcement agents did not swell, in America at least. At the time of this writing, only 15 percent of active duty police officers identified themselves as women, and women made up just 20 percent of FBI agents. This is despite what retired FBI agent and University of Northern Florida professor Ellen Glasser points out: "Half of criminal justice students in college are women."

The common explanation for why is a simple one, as another former FBI agent put it to me: Generally speaking, women do not have the same strength as men.

For better or worse, this is a biology thing, not an equality thing. The Centers for Disease Control's most recent data found that 89 percent of adult men are stronger than 89 percent of adult women. The *Journal of Applied Physiology* reports that men have an average of 40 percent more upper-body strength than women. And if two random strangers of the opposite sex decide to have a leg-kicking contest on the street, there's only a tiny chance that the woman will win.

The following chart shows the grip strength, a common proxy for overall strength, of men versus women by age:

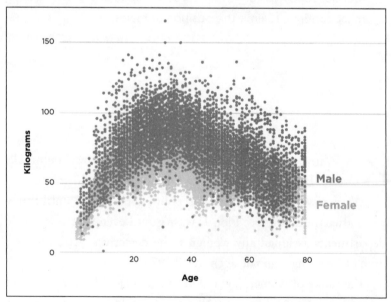

Data via Centers for Disease Control

Genetics says that women are not going to be as good at chasing bad guys, punching bad guys, or intimidating bad guys with their size. That's one of the reasons that FBI director J. Edgar Hoover didn't let women become agents at all. "The Special Agent in his appearance, approach, and conduct must create the impression to his adversary that among other qualities he is intrepid, forceful, aggressive, dominant, and resolute," Hoover wrote. The other reason for excluding females was unity. Hoover's army of agents needed to march to the same beat to be an effective team. "We must put up the best front possible," he explained.

And you know what? That's okay. It turns out that some jobs, like law enforcement, are just better suited for men. Kate Warne was nothing but a rare anomaly of a female on a law enforcement Dream Team. She is by far the exception to the rule.

Except, it turns out that Hoover was wrong, and all that stuff in those last two paragraphs is garbage.

The story of FBI special agent Chris Jung and a Newark mafia boss shows us why.

5.

The morning sun reflected off the garbage floating in the bend of the Passaic River that formed the city limits of Newark, New Jersey. Horns blared and street hustlers hustled as bell-bottomed commuters poured into the cluster of office buildings on the river's western shore. Inside one of those buildings, agents from the Federal Bureau of Investigation were planning a raid.

Well, sort of. They were planning something. They weren't sure what.

Newark in the 1970s was run by syndicates of a handful of

Italian American crime families. The Lucchese family was known for controlling the newspaper delivery and kosher meat unions. The Genovese family was famous for its founder, "Lucky" Luciano. And then of course there was the DeCavalcante crime family, whose de facto boss is said to be the basis for the character Tony in HBO's *The Sopranos*. They controlled the city's gambling parlors, its piers, its garbage collection, and its murder.

Mafia bosses are hard to get into a courtroom. But in the spring of '74, the FBI had dug up some dirt involving one of the big bosses. (The FBI agents I interviewed were willing to tell me this story but not the name of which mob boss it was. So we'll just call him Mr. Lombardi.)

The dirt was dirty enough to subpoena Lombardi, or force him to appear in court to testify.

But there was a problem. The law required that subpoenas be delivered in person, by hand. Once you received the subpoena, you're required by law to appear in court, or you could be arrested. And if you were a mob boss who appeared in court, you were suddenly in a lot of danger. Of saying something you shouldn't—or worse, of another mobster getting worried that you were going to.

The mob had figured out by this time that one of the best ways to stay out of prison or the Passaic was to avoid being summoned to court in the first place. If a subpoena never got delivered, it couldn't be enforced. So they'd developed a simple, but effective strategy: surround the boss with enough layers of bodyguards that no cop could ever talk to him in person. Thus, the Newark crime heads of the 1970s were able to move about town in style and yet remain untouchable.

Lombardi knew the FBI would love to see him in court, so his operation kept special track of the agents in Newark's organized crime squad. And anyone a mafia guard didn't know would get stopped upon approach, until identity was verified and permission granted.

Agents at the bureau had been scratching their heads for weeks about how to get close enough to Lombardi to deliver the subpoena. They'd tried ambushing him while he was out at lunch, but bodyguards had blocked the way. They needed a better plan.

A dozen special agents and the supervisor of the Organized Crime Squad had convened in a war room to brainstorm new ideas. They had decided that there needed to be some sort of raid. The problem is that a subpoena is a request, not an arrest. You can't really deliver a subpoena at gunpoint because you can't shoot someone for preventing you from delivering paperwork.

Around and around the agents went. Every idea for how to coerce, intimidate, or blast their way past Lombardi's bodyguards was a no-go.

That's when the rookie from another department, Chris Jung, raised her hand. The Organized Crime Squad had invited her as a guest because they were out of ideas. They were willing to consider almost anything at this point.

The male agents turned their heads when she spoke up. "Mr. Lombardi's daughter is getting married in two weeks," she pointed out.

And that gave her an idea.

Two weeks later, a chauffeured black car pulled up to the wedding palace where the Lombardi family was celebrating their daughter's reception. Out of the car stepped an elegant woman in heels and a purple high-necked gown.

The security guards couldn't help but notice Ms. Jung as she walked confidently into the reception hall. Like she had predicted at the squad meeting, the guards did nothing to stop her. That a gorgeously dressed woman like her might be a federal agent occurred to no one on an occasion like this. None of the staff questioned whether she'd been invited.

Once inside, the job was simple. Jung made a beeline to the front of the reception line, where the happy couple and their families greeted guests. The bride looked beautiful. Next to her, the father of the bride—Mr. Lombardi himself—beamed.

Until Jung stepped in front of him and handed him the subpoena papers.

"Enjoy your night," she said.

The man stared at her as she turned and walked out. As she exited the building, the mob boss began to howl.

The chauffeur, a fellow special agent, was waiting with the engine running. "I think I ruined the wedding," Jung said.

Anticlimactic? Yes. But that, it turns out, is key.

6.

Here's a statistic that might surprise you. Women make up 12 percent of American cops but only 2 percent of police shootings.*

---

*Here I should point out that gender is not binary, neither identity-wise nor anatomically. But police department data—and most of American demographic studies, for that matter—almost always identify people as either male, female, or "prefer not to answer." Since the best demographic research at the time of this writing found that less than half a percent of Americans identify as nonbinary or transgender, we've not enough data to focus on or make hard conclusions about anything but the male/female binary. As we'll see by the end of this chapter, however, the meta-idea we're exploring applies beyond the binary.

Curiously, this doesn't seem to lower the success rates of female officers. Cop for cop, women seem to be just as good at stopping crimes as men.

It's just that female cops are six times less likely to shoot someone.

Even more dramatic, female officers are eight times less likely to use excessive force than male officers, according to studies by the National Center for Women and Policing. Police partnerships with female officers in them make fewer mistakes and, on average, solve problems with less collateral damage.

Wearing a fancy dress to deliver a subpoena doesn't sound nearly as exciting as a SWAT team raid. Neither does putting a floppy hat on a congressman for a midnight train ride. But both of our stories about female crime fighters erode a common misconception about law enforcement: that the job is about bullets and muscle.

It turns out that fighting crime usually isn't about fighting at all. We could cherry-pick all sorts of anecdotes about times when the day was saved by cops literally punching people (as television often depicts), but what happened in the case of the FBI and Mr. Lombardi is how it works most of the time. "The nature of the work," says former FBI assistant director Janice Fedarcyk, is primarily about "good judgment and problem-solving skills." And according to FBI reports, women in police departments and intelligence bureaus are on average more successful than men at de-escalating dangerous situations without the use of force.

All of this begs a couple of questions, however: If it's true that law enforcement is about good judgment and problem solving, why would women tend to screw up less than men? Men are intelligent, too. Furthermore, if it's true that women do so well at this kind of work, why do we still have so few female law enforcement agents?

It turns out that both of these questions have the same answer.

On former US Bureau of Alcohol, Tobacco, Firearms and Explosives assistant director Kathleen Kiernan's office desk sits a closed padlock. It's there for an analogy she's used hundreds of times when explaining why women succeed in law enforcement.

If she hands you the padlock and asks you to break into it, she says that more often than not, "Men will figure out how to tactically compromise it, break it, subvert it, all those kinds of things."

But instead of trying to physically tackle the lock, she says, most women will initially try to find the key or figure out a way to psychologically compromise the person who has it.

This, Kiernan insists, is the way most women in law enforcement work. Most of them haven't spent their lives assuming they can default to muscles to solve problems, so they use tools like negotiation and communication before they resort to force. And often that turns out to be a better way.*

During her thirty years at the NYPD, Denise Thomas, one of the first black women to become a Brooklyn homicide detective, was revered by fellow cops. She policed high school violence, solved decades-old murder cases, and busted bad guys in the Marcy Projects back when JAY-Z was there selling crack. And most of the time, she told me, it was psychological work. "You have to have a knack for dealing with people," she says. The job is not to fight, but to disarm the fight. "You have to defuse the situation and talk them down."

---

*This is the same reason, in fact, that studies show that, despite tending to have less upper-body strength, women tend to make better rock climbers than men.

Agent after agent, cop after cop told me variations on this same theme. As a young local police officer, Fedarcyk* told me, it became clear to her that because "women do not have the same upper-body strength as men, I had to develop my communication skills to learn to deflate a situation that could escalate."†

Think back to Chris Jung and the mob boss. The male agents went in circles trying to come up with ways to barge their way through Mr. Lombardi's bodyguards. And Jung put on a ball gown and walked right in. It was an obvious strategy in retrospect, but it never occurred to the men. To the one woman in the room, it was a no-brainer.

So why don't more women make the leap from criminal justice school to law enforcement? Some said the reason was women don't think they're going to be able to beat men up. Others said women dislike the boys'-club culture that surrounds law enforcement or the violent ethos of American law enforcement generally. But not being able to beat men up is also exactly what helps women to fight crime smarter.

And that's not because female officers are bad with guns. In fact, during the Lombardi case, Jung happened to be the number one marksman in the FBI. She was the first to get a perfect score on the FBI's timed firearms test and became the head firearms instructor for the bureau.

---

*At the time I interviewed her, Fedarcyk held the record of the highest-ranking female FBI agent.

†Before we keep going, we need to step back for a second and note that these statistics we've been discussing about men and women are true in general, but not of every individual out there. Many women are terrible negotiators. Many male police officers are thoughtful, non-aggressive communicators who would never punch a pillow. We're not saying that one's gender will mean that one has the characteristics we're discussing. We're just saying that they will be much more likely to than not. Gender, in this case, is proxy for probability. But as we'll soon see, predicting behavior from demographics is not the most important thing afoot here.

Despite this, in her mind, firearms were simply part of a larger strategic tool kit. "We probably are more prone to pull a gun than a man would be," Jung says, "but not necessarily to use it."*

While I was interviewing all these detectives about their teamwork dynamics, American newspaper headlines were reporting a depressing amount of police violence. Good cops were being killed. Bad cops were killing unarmed people. Race and hate were often factors in both. The country was experiencing a backlash to a state of overreach, and good people on both sides of the badge were suffering.

In this violent context, everything we've explored so far leads to an inevitable conclusion. If we want to do a better job at law enforcement and reduce violence, the simplest solution is to make all our law enforcement officers women. All indications say that crime-fighting organizations would get better if they got rid of the men.

Except no. If we did that, it turns out, we'd have another problem.

7.

Pretend that you are having a housewarming party, and you've invited your eight best friends. You've baked a delicious round cake, and because you love your friends equally, you want to cut it into eight equal pieces for them.

---

*And then she laughed and said, "There's something very frightening to most men when they see a woman with a loaded gun."

But there's a catch: the knife you are using, for whatever reason, is going to break after you make three cuts. How do you slice the cake into eight equal pieces in just three moves?

If you're like most people, you probably first cut the cake in half vertically:

Then you cut it in half horizontally:

And then, again, if you're like most people, you'll start making a third and final cut diagonally before realizing that this only makes six slices of cake:

So what do you do?

At this point, you might try to get fancy and diagram out some funny-looking cake slices, but then you'll remember that the pieces have to be equal for your friends to know you love them the same.

There is a simple answer, though. It just requires changing your point of view.

The solution is to go ahead and make the first two cuts, creating four slices of cake, and then to turn your head and look at the cake sideways:

And cut it all the way through.

This little puzzle illustrates something important. It shows us in a very literal way a simple truth, that sometimes the best way to solve a problem requires looking at it from a different angle. In other words, to change perspective.*

---

*In technical terms, perspective is the way we map the world around us to our own "internal language." For example, when a geologist hears the word "rock," her perspective might make her first think of something different from when a teenager hears the word "rock." In less vocabulary-centric terms, perspective is the angle from which we consider things.

Perspective is built by how we uniquely experience the world. A bystander who sees a building on fire might perceive what's happening very differently from a firefighter, or from a person who once had his house burn down. When you ask tall people what makes for a good airline, most of them will tell you "legroom," while short people will tell you "elbow room." Neither answer is incorrect in this case, depending on whether you see the world from six inches higher off the ground.

Perspective is one dimension of every person's mental tool kit. To introduce the other dimension, we return to our housewarming party for another puzzle.

Pretend that next to the cake at your kitchen table are six glasses lined up in a row. The first three glasses are full of milk. The next three are empty. Like so:

Now, say I asked you to move the glasses so that the full and empty cups alternate. But there's a catch: you can only move one glass.

Can you do it?

For most people, this one is a bigger head-scratcher than the cake. Most of us try to move the second glass of milk to sit in

between two empty glasses, only to realize that it still leaves two full glasses next to each other.

If you're still stumped, try this:

Pretend that I asked you to solve this same puzzle, but that I also told you to pretend that you had to use the technique of a chemist to do it.

If you were stumped before, at this point the answer may have suddenly become obvious.

Pour the milk from the second glass into the second to last glass, and put the glass back.

This puzzle helps us understand the second dimension of a person's mental tool kit: something called heuristics. If perspective is how we see a problem, heuristics are how we go about solving it. You can think of heuristics as "rules of thumb" or problem-solving strategies.

The way a chemist's brain instinctively attempts the milk puzzle is likely going to be different than the way, say, a forklift operator's brain does. This isn't to say that forklift operators wouldn't be able to solve the milk puzzle. What it says is that if you move objects around all day with a forklift, your first strategy for rearranging glasses of milk is likely going to be different than if your job is to pour liquids in and out of containers all day.

These two parts of our mental tool kit—perspective and heuristics—go hand in hand. And they explain what's actually important when it comes to working together in law enforcement—and what's really at play in our study of gender and cops.

To understand what I mean, let's look at the following diagram of a mountain range:

RANGE OF POTENTIAL SOLUTIONS

This mountain range represents the set of potential solutions to a hypothetical problem. Each peak represents a different solution. The higher the peak, the better the solution. Every problem in life or work can be represented by its own unique mountain range like this, with varying quality of solutions.

As you can see, some solutions to our hypothetical problem are not as good as others. And in this case there is one best solution— the highest peak in the middle.

Unfortunately, when we're exploring real problems, it is as if we're hiking through fog. We can't actually see the entire mountain range. This means that when we find a peak—a solution that works—we don't know if we're at the top of the range or just the top of one mountain. We have to decide whether to continue exploring for a better solution.

And here's where our cake analogy comes back. Where we start out on the mountain—and what part of it we can see—depends on our perspective. It's like getting dropped off by helicopter at a particular spot on the range:

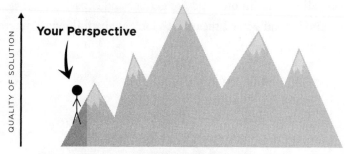

Now that we're here, we need a strategy—or heuristic—to help us explore for solutions.

Let's say you have one mountain heuristic, and it is to march in one direction until the mountain stops going up, and then to climb down the other side for five hundred paces. If the slope turns back uphill by then, you keep hiking upward until you reach the next peak. But if you go downhill for five hundred paces and the slope keeps going down, you turn around and hike up to the last highest point you found.

As we can see, your perspective and heuristic helped you find a decent solution, but little did you know there were other, better solutions out there.

This is where teamwork can help. Say you're working with someone who shares a similar perspective on the problem you're working on. He'll get dropped off at the same place on the mountain range as you originally did.

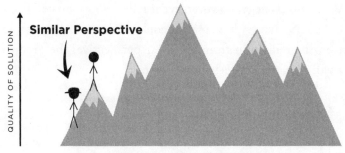

RANGE OF POTENTIAL SOLUTIONS

But let's say that your teammate has a different mountain-climbing heuristic than yours. His strategy is to hike until he reaches the trough between two mountains, and then to go up whichever one is steepest. Using this technique, he might continue past you and find that the next mountain over has a higher peak.

It turns out that our teammate's diverse heuristic allowed him to find a better solution. He then calls down from his mountain peak at this point, and you join him.

This is how group work often happens. Whoever in the group has the best heuristic will eventually find the best solution, and the group (hopefully) follows it. This is why we put people with different specialties together—such as pairing a design expert and a programming expert together to build a website.

With this strategy, however, eventually your group will run into a problem. No matter how many people are in your crew, if you all start on the mountain from a similar perspective, the group will eventually get stuck together on one peak.

But this is where something interesting can happen.

When you introduce someone with a different perspective, it's like she is getting dropped off on a different part of the mountain range altogether. She sees it from a point of view that the rest of the group doesn't.

So let's say this happens. One of your team members shows up with a very different perspective of your mountain range. Even if she has the same heuristics as you (say you went to mountain climbing school together) and explores the mountain using your "five hundred

paces" strategy, she might end up finding a better solution simply because she started in a different place.

But even if she doesn't end up finding a better solution than the rest of the group, her vantage point offers the group an opportunity. The group can now play with different combinations of perspectives and heuristics to test if there are higher peaks to be found. In this case, the heuristic of hiking to the trough and going up the steep way, combined with the new perspective, reveals the highest peak in the range.

Thus, the whole group is able to get to a solution that nobody would have found on his or her own. The *ne plus ultra* of the mountain range.

This is the math, as it were, behind the concept of "synergy." The combination of diverse mental tool kits—looking at the cake sideways and moving the milk glasses differently—leads to the potential for a group to do better than the sum of its parts. It explains how a whole squad of smart people who think the same is less likely to find a higher peak on the mountain than a group of people who think differently. And it's our first hint at why some police partnerships outwit more bad guys, and how teams like the Russian Five can beat competitors with better individual statistics.

Most great sports teams tend to rely on players having a diversity of skills in order to specialize in different positions, but as any expert or athlete will tell you, the difference between skilled athletes and world champions is not about who's bigger or stronger. Just as it is with cops, world-class performance often comes down to an athlete's *mental game*. The Red Army were great at hitting a hockey puck, but the way they *thought* together was different from other teams. Their style, their problem solving, their "mind reading" made a difference for the team. It's not hard to see how Coach Tarasov's ninja-hockey style, combined with Coach Tikhonov's toughness, led a whole generation of players to play on a taller mountain peak than their peers.

The mountain analogy we just walked through comes from an acclaimed professor named Dr. Scott Page, who teaches "complex systems" at the University of Michigan. His research findings, from years of studying group dynamics, are conclusive: teams with diverse mental tool kits consistently outperform groups of "the best and the brightest."*

Let's put this together. By now we've seen that problem-solving smarts—not physical toughness—is key to a successful police squad.

---

*Scientists like Dr. Page have developed mathematical proofs that bear this out. Just as mixing different colors of paint can create new colors, mixing different perspectives and heuristics can lead to new solutions to problems.

And problem-solving smarts are going to be a function of that squad's "cognitive diversity," its diversity of perspectives and heuristics.

Unlike some jobs where we want to just climb the same one mountain over and over—say, an assembly line—solving and preventing crimes is almost always a new, custom mountain problem. This is why adding women to law enforcement changes things, but it's also why it wouldn't be such a great idea if we suddenly made all cops and FBI agents women.

If every law enforcement partnership looked like Charlie's Angels, we might indeed increase the negotiation skill of a lot of departments. But we'd also be shooting those departments in the foot (a thing male cops occasionally do*). No men at all would mean increasing law enforcement's likelihood of getting stuck on suboptimal mountain peaks on the other side of the range. We need lots of perspectives if we want to give our officers the best chance at solving hard problems. (And as someone who loses his keys a lot, I've learned that once in a while a team needs a guy with a good heuristic for kicking down a door.)

At this point, our discussion begs a rather obvious, but important question: Is gender the only kind of difference that leads to cognitive diversity in police work?

The answer is absolutely not. And this brings us to an important subject to step back and discuss before continuing. As we've discovered, cognitive diversity is a key element of teams that exceed the sums of their parts. But the term "diversity" itself is a tricky one, and we need to talk about it for a moment.

"Diversity" technically just means "variety," but the word has

---

*I dare not give a URL, but YouTube is rife with examples. And those are just the ones caught on camera!

become a euphemism—especially in America—for one thing: race.*
It's the term many people† use to refer to race when they are too
uncomfortable to come out and say it. And since race is still very
much a hot-button topic, "diversity" has in turn become a word that
makes a lot of people nervous.

Reality is, "diversity" doesn't mean race. Nor does it mean gender, the second-most frequent thing people think when they hear
the word.

Because it's such a charged term, though, I'm going to use the
word "difference" in this book as a catchall whenever I generally mean
two or more things that are not the same. Whenever I use the word
"diversity" from here on, I'll try to pair it with an adjective for specific-
ity. Like "demographic diversity" or "diversity of shoe sizes."‡ It's a good
habit that I'd encourage you to pick up, too, if you don't already do it.

Now that we've explored the power of cognitive diversity, things
are about to get interesting. But we need to be cautious about one
more thing before we proceed.

Some people will be tempted to take our lesson in perspectives

---

*Sorry, but it's getting harder to type with Peanuts, my restless fifteen-thousand-pound bull
elephant, in the room.

I'm a Caucasian American male who grew up with more opportunities than most other
people in the world. I neither possess the understanding and authority to resolve matters of
most kinds of discrimination, nor can I make sense of the horrific atrocities that scar my own
nation's past. This book is no sop for centuries of injustice, and I can't personally relate to
the suffering of people who have gone through things that I haven't. So I'm not going to
pretend to.

The good news is, the study of human collaboration is a scientific discipline like any
other, and we're going to explore it as such. Hopefully some of the things we discuss in this
book can help us attack problems of injustice together. A better "we" needs both you and
me, so thanks for being here, and for trusting my intentions.

†Data show that white people tend to be the most uncomfortable speaking in non-
euphemistic terms about race. For example, a 2016 study by the Pew Research Center found
that only 8 percent of Caucasians talk directly about race on social media, while black social
media users talk about it four times as much.

‡We won't actually talk about shoe sizes in this book, but we will talk about foot blisters!

and heuristics and use it to jump over other types of differences—or even use it as an excuse to say that demographic diversity like race or gender *doesn't* matter. That's a bad idea. It's a temptation we need to resist, and here's why:

The most accurate way to predict cognitive diversity would be to open up someone's head and poke around inside their neural makeup. But because we are not James Bond villains, we have to look for proxies for different thinking instead. We need to be able to make our best guess, based on other clues.

Our perspectives and heuristics come from our life's experiences. Our neural pathways form as we live through stuff. So, the more we can identify differences in life experience, the more we can predict cognitive diversity.

Some of those experiences are obvious to spot: We studied different subjects, at different schools. We grew up in different kinds of towns. We had that crazy thing happen to us that one time.

But we can go deeper than that. Our brains are shaped every day by all the micro-experiences we have, and those are affected by the way we see the world and ourselves. And how we see the world and ourselves is affected deeply by how the world sees and treats us. So, when we have a group of people who look different, or identify themselves differently in some ways, we can guess that they may think differently in some ways, too.

In other words, if you and I are a different age or race or gender, it's highly likely that we have experienced life differently. People look at us differently. They speak to us differently. They invite us to do different things. They include us—or exclude us—at different times. And in some cases like height, age, or physical ability, we may literally see things differently. Sometimes those different experiences are subtle, and sometimes they're more blatant. But they slowly form a mosaic of mental wiring. That mosaic shapes our perspective and beliefs—how we define and predict things—and helps us develop our heuristics and skills—how we approach and deal with things.*

So, it turns out that demographic differences end up being pretty good predictors of differences on the inside:

External & Internal Attributes
Age, Gender, Race, Sexual Orientation, Habits, Physical Ability, Ethnicity, Appearance, Religion, Parental Status, Marital Status, Personal Preferences, Geographic Background, Economic Background...

Life Experiences
Day-to-Day Experiences, Education, Work, Travel, Locations Lived, Microaggressions, Micro-Opportunities, People Met...

Cognitive Mosaic
Perspectives, Heuristics, "How You Roll"

Let's use another hypothetical scenario to illustrate how proxies for cognitive diversity work in practice:

Pretend that it's the year 2010, and you're making a movie starring Tom Hanks. At the last minute before you start filming, Tom tells you he can't do the movie anymore. Whom do you replace him with?

---

*It's important to note that, eventually, having a different perspective often leads to developing a different heuristic. Someone who sees the cake sideways will probably develop a different cutting technique than someone who only sees it from the top. This is not guaranteed; but it is likely.

This is a question that Dr. Page likes to ask his University of Michigan students. But I'm a geek, so I decided to ask several thousand American adults whom they'd pick in this same scenario. I collected answers online and then sorted them by the responders' races.

White people chose a wide variety of Hanks replacements: Josh Brolin, Harrison Ford, Hugh Grant, Brad Pitt, and (my favorite) Ryan Gosling were common. Robert Downey Jr. received a slight plurality of votes, and Tom Hanks's son Colin gathered a high percentage, too.

Black people, however, picked the same person 52 percent of the time: Denzel Washington.

It turns out that, race aside, Hanks and Washington are two of the most similar actors in Hollywood. They're about the same age and height. They have similar demeanors and are longtime family men. They're versatile performers and winners of the same kinds of awards. Each has done funny movies but is not a comedian. Each has done both blockbusters and Oscar bait. They even get paid about the same.

In fact, Denzel Washington may just be the best fill-in for Tom Hanks in Hollywood. As with our cake puzzle, this is obvious once you see it. But it's easier to see it from the perspective of a black person than a white person.

To be clear, being black doesn't mean you will pick Denzel. There's just a much higher chance that you will pick him than a white person will. Once again, what makes the difference is the way you think, which has to do with all the little things you've lived through.*

---

*My friend Eric, who's Mexican American, provides us with an excellent example of how our mental mosaic can be shaped by all sorts of experiences. "I'm multilingual," he says. "So even if you speak Mandarin, English, and Swahili, I can relate to you because I know what it is like to think in one language and dream in another." Despite their different races, Eric says in many ways he thinks more like director George Lucas than he thinks like many Latin Americans. He and Lucas both grew up in Modesto, California. Depending on the Problem Mountain range, adding Eric to a group of black and white Northern Californians might not increase cognitive diversity very much, even though he's Latino. But adding him to a group of locals in Mexico City might.

Our life experiences add up to what legendary leadership transformation coach Keith Yamashita of SYPartners calls "how we roll." Basically, this is our operating style: the day-to-day application of our unique mental mosaics.* Yamashita says that great teams take time to understand as much as possible about how their members roll: How do they learn best? Do they do their best original work in the morning or afternoon? How do they like to manage their time? What do they need in order to thrive? How do they argue? What are their biggest strengths, their superpowers?[†]

Then, anytime we face a challenge, Yamashita suggests stepping back and doing two things: "First, take a moment to frame the problem." Is it a routine problem? Does it require breaking new ground? How high are the stakes? Routine problems don't require much (or often, any) cognitive diversity, while novel problems benefit from it greatly. "Based on that," Yamashita says, "do a casting session." He uses the word "casting" deliberately. A movie director doesn't just grab whoever's around or whoever was in the last movie she made. The cast for every movie needs to make sense for the plot and script.

Understanding "how we roll" not only helps team members to appreciate each other's differences, but it also becomes a pragmatic way to figure out who might best contribute their mental tool kit. "I might be a gay, Asian dad, which is true," says Yamashita, but a more relevant difference in a particular situation might be, "I'm a morning person." Or, "I'm very empathetic."

When we start to think about team building as casting, we start

---

*For decades, Yamashita has helped CEOs like Steve Jobs, Howard Schultz, and Oprah Winfrey fundamentally change the way they work with their teams by, among other things, teaching them how to put cognitive diversity to work. He's also one of the most delightful people you'll ever meet.

[†]You can learn more about Yamashita's process at shanesnow.com/dreamteams/superpowers.

to think of our differences as gifts, rather than statistics and numbers. "It's not a Noah's Ark mentality," Yamashita says. We don't need *every* kind of person in *every* meeting. The casting director's question is, "What group of people will give us the best shot at a breakthrough?" The most exciting part of this puzzle is not simply putting different kinds of people on the mountain range together, though. It's what happens to them next.

8.

In 2013, professors from four US universities got 186 Americans who identified themselves as Republicans and Democrats—two groups that tend to think differently about many things—to read a murder mystery. Each person was told to prepare to come debate the answer to the mystery with someone who disagreed with them. Half of the people were told that they would be debating with a member of the other political party. Half were told they would debate with someone from their own party.

And then something interesting happened.

It turned out that Republicans who were told that a Democrat would be debating the case with them prepared more clever arguments. And Democrats who went up against Republicans did, too. Even though the topic had nothing to do with politics.

The study concluded that being put together to work on something with people with different viewpoints "jolts us into cognitive action" that we don't get when we work with people who we assume share our perspective. "Simply interacting with individuals who are different forces group members to prepare better, to anticipate alternative viewpoints and to expect that reaching consensus will take effort," writes one of the study's authors, Dr. Katherine W. Phillips, vice dean at Columbia Business School. "Simply adding social diversity to a group makes people *believe* that differences of perspective might exist among them and that belief makes people change their behavior. [Italics in original]"*

This is one reason why research studies from McKinsey & Company and Catalyst Group show that the more diverse thinkers in a company's higher ranks, especially its boardroom, the more likely it is to come up with strategies that turn higher profits and avoid making stupid mistakes—like buying bad companies.† It's also a reason why cities with more immigrants from different parts of the world tend to produce more patents. People think more critically when when different people are around.

If you've got a group of people planning how to remodel a building, and a person in a wheelchair rolls in to join the planning session, everyone is suddenly going to think a little bit differently about the project.

Or when, say, a masculine group of law enforcement agents brings in women as collaborators, the men will suddenly begin to think more critically about the challenges at hand.

And, it turns out, vice versa.

---

*Here's a fun bit of research on police dyads that goes the other direction than what we've been focusing on. A classic study published in the Journal of Policing and Safety shows us that female cops benefit from having male partners, too. Women in mixed-gender police duos have more confidence in their work and recall details from suspect situations more accurately.

†Other factors that lead to fewer wrongful police shootings and bad business deals, according to various studies: having a mix of age diversity in the room, having a mix of straight and openly gay team members, and having people who are both parents and not each increases such groups' chances of better decisions.

9.

When Kate Warne first walked into Allan Pinkerton's office in Chicago for an interview in 1856, Pinkerton assumed she was there for a secretary position. To his surprise, Warne—who was around twenty-three at the time—declared that she was responding to his newspaper advertisement for detectives.

Widowed at a young age, Warne had learned how to fend for herself in the tough streets of Chicago. She knew she had unique skills the detective agency could use.

But, Pinkerton exclaimed, "It is not the custom to employ women detectives!"

Warne knew. What she lacked in brawn she would make up in cleverness, she insisted. Women, she said, had an eye for detail and were patient. Plus, Warne argued, she could be "most useful in worming out secrets in many places which would be impossible for a male detective."

Pinkerton thought about it that night. Despite the objections of his associates, he hired Warne the next day.

He didn't regret it. Warne proved to be one of his most capable agents. "She has never let me down," Pinkerton later said. And she changed the dynamic of the entire agency.

We should take note that there were two areas of advantage that Warne's gender brought to detective work. The first was external. As a woman, she could walk under a bad guy's nose without suspicion—much like Chris Jung did at the mob wedding. But second and more important, Warne brought a different way of thinking to Pinkerton's enterprise—just like Jung helped the FBI come up with cleverer plans because she thought differently. Warne's skill at disguises and logistical maneuvering was instrumental in saving Lincoln.

Warne changed the way Pinkerton thought about detective work and helped him build the most successful private detective agency in history—an agency that would lay the groundwork for the Federal Secret Service.* Because of Warne, Pinkerton made his company logo an eye with the words "We never sleep" underneath it—a nod to her having stayed up all night watching Lincoln. This trademark caught the public imagination and became the origin of the term "private eye."

Together, Warne, Webster, and Pinkerton formed a Dream Team. The agency, and those three in particular, went on to shape the private detective industry as it's known today.

Warne's contribution to Pinkerton's firm was so valuable (one newspaper called her the best detective in America "—maybe the world") that Pinkerton had her build a department he called the Female Detective Bureau, whose job was to supply women agents to collaborate on

---

*Tragically, the legislation that would create the Secret Service was on Lincoln's desk the day he was assassinated.

various male agents' cases. Pinkerton wanted a Dream Team working on every one of his cases. The women and men remained in segregated hierarchies within the agency—reflecting the backward social norms of the nineteenth century—but the mere inclusion of women in detective work was remarkably forward thinking for Pinkerton's time. More important to Pinkerton, including female agents this way was brilliant for solving cases.

He had been convinced of the power of cognitive diversity.

Coincidentally, the most notable proponent of cognitive diversity at the time was, in fact, President Lincoln.* How Lincoln convinced his biggest ideological rivals to work with him in the White House has been well chronicled in books and films. Lincoln knew that his team's different ways of thinking gave him his best shot at winning the Civil War and keeping the nation intact.

If only more presidents after him had understood that.

So far, we've seen how people can do extraordinary things together by combining cognitive diversity. You'll notice how each Dream Team member we've met so far brought a different tool kit to her or his respective collaboration. Warne and Webster contributed very different things to Pinkerton's Dream Team of detectives. Though they played like they could read each other's minds, our Soviet hockey players each brought very different things to the rink with

---

*Side note: At the time of this writing, Lincoln was also the first of two US presidents known to have impersonated a handicapped person. One did so to avoid an attempted assassination; the other, we might say, did so as an act of character assassination.

them, too. And it's not a stretch to say that the Red Army reigned because of the combination of their coaches' heuristics and perspectives—Tarasov's radical creativity and Tikhonov's ferocity. There is still much more to piece together in our quest to understand Dream Teams, but as we've seen, without different mental tool kits, we limit how high up the mountain we can go.

Notice how this runs counter to the advice that we tend to get in many of our organizations. *Get more people like that on the bus!* we say. *Let's double down on our strengths!* we proclaim. *Let's not hire her; she's not a culture fit!* we advise.

Unless you're recruiting an army of hammer swingers to break rocks on an assembly line, this kind of advice is profoundly stupid. What does "fit" get us but homogeneous thinking? What does collecting carbon copies of ourselves do but stick more people on the same mountain peak?

"If you see your job and your work as primarily known things or small increments . . . [cognitive diversity] is not that important," says Yamashita. But breaking new ground, he says, by nature "requires different angles, different ideas, different ways of doing it, different backgrounds, different sensitivities, different layers, different slices."

Indeed, breakthroughs happen when we break the mold.

We've learned that when it comes to making progress together, the differences that matter most are the ones inside our heads. And those differences are built by our experiences, which in turn are shaped by who we are.

Knowing this is good news for a couple of reasons. First, it gives us a concrete reason to collaborate with people who aren't like us—a utilitarian excuse to be inclusive, which also happens to be a good moral choice.

It also helps us know what kinds of things to look for when building teams to solve problems together: different perspectives and heuristics, and the things that are proxy for them—experiences, identity, and biology. This gives us the foundation for the rest of our teamwork exploration.*

But before we get to all of that—and to the other crucial factors that make regular teams into Dream Teams—we have something pressing to sort out.

If we're going to conclude that our differences and the cognitive diversity that flows from them make us smarter together, then it turns out that we have a problem.

Why do differences almost always make groups worse?

---

*It also hints at the skill set that we can develop as individuals if we want to get better at solving problems ourselves. The mountain analogy applies just as well within our own heads as among groups. People who can think through lots of perspectives and heuristics at once have higher chances of finding a solution for tough problems than others. As F. Scott Fitzgerald famously declared, "The test of a first-rate intelligence is the ability to hold two opposing ideas in mind at the same time." Learning to do that—to train ourselves to become open-minded and find new perspectives—wouldn't just make us better collaborators. It would make us smarter ourselves. After all, says Dr. Page, "We did not get the theory of relativity from a crowd. We got it from a diverse, novel thinker in a patent office."

ZWEI

TROUBLE IN SHAOLIN

*"We wanted to make money.
We wanted to get outta the streets."*

1.

In May 1998, two massive worlds collided.

Chrysler, the Detroit-based maker of Dodges and Jeeps, had the highest profit margins of any auto company in the world. Its product development cost was half of Ford's, and one-third of General Motors's—even though it was the smallest of the three companies.

Despite this, CEO Bob Eaton worried that Chrysler wasn't prepared for the future. As the Internet empowered people with more information, car buyers demanded higher quality. Advances in electronics threatened to make Chrysler's engine designs obsolete. And a surge of cheaper and superior Toyotas and Lexuses imperiled the jobs of Chrysler's 123,000 blue-collar workers.

Daimler, meanwhile, was one of Europe's top manufacturing companies. The three hundred thousand employees of this Germany-based maker of Mercedes-Benz and Maybach built some of the nicest cars, trucks, and buses in the world. Though Daimler was on the cutting edge of automotive design, CEO Jürgen Schrempp was worried, too. Daimler pumped millions into research and development but was having trouble making a big return on its investments. The company had a tiny market share in the United States, and it, too, feared mounting competition from Japanese automakers.

The two CEOs realized that their companies' heuristics might cancel out each other's weaknesses. Chrysler's unbeatable efficiency plus Daimler's legendary innovation? Killer combo. Daimler's quality and Chrysler's "cowboy can-do" would make them unstoppable. Combined, they'd have the tools and talent to take on Ford, GM, and Toyota, and to become one of—if not *the*—biggest automobile companies on the planet.

So they made a deal. Eaton and Schrempp shook hands, and Daimler and Chrysler became DaimlerChrysler. Schrempp called it "a merger of equals, a merger of growth, and a merger of unprecedented strength."

The new company was worth around 100 billion dollars. It was the largest transcontinental merger in corporate history.

And it would go down as one of corporate history's biggest disasters.

According to the *Harvard Business Review*, between 70 and 90 percent of company mergers fail to achieve synergy. That is, they don't manage to eventually turn two companies into one business that's worth more than the sum of the individual companies' value before the merger. More alarming, half of mergers actually result in a worse business.

Few cases of this are as dramatic as DaimlerChrysler. Three years after the "merger of unprecedented strength," the 100-billion-dollar company was worth somewhere between 44 and 48 billion—about what Daimler had been worth by itself.

It was supposed to be the greatest merger ever. A Dream Team of automakers. What happened?

The colossal failure has been the subject of many business school case studies. Some point to how the two companies overestimated their potential. Others illustrate how management stumbles hampered growth.

But those things alone didn't wipe out 50 billion dollars in value. DaimlerChrysler didn't crash because their cars got worse. Or because its managers forgot how to do their jobs. The cause of DaimlerChrysler's epic tumble is the same thing that's doomed the majority of mergers in modern business history.

The merger failed because of "cultural conflict."

On the surface, Daimler's and Chrysler's people were very similar. They were four hundred thousand mostly male, mostly white engineers and designers and assembly-line workers and managers who loved cars.

"They look like us, they talk like us, they're focused on the same things, and their command of English is impeccable," said one Chrysler executive of his German counterparts, as reported in a Dartmouth case study. "There was definitely no culture clash."

This assessment was laughably superficial.

The Germans and Americans who were now supposed to work together had different communication habits, different concepts of personal space, and different negotiation tactics. They had different core beliefs about women in the workplace and the role of leadership. They had different levels of intensity, different motivations, and different perspectives on what mattered when it came to making cars. In other words, they had, as we learned in the last chapter, significant diversity of perspectives and heuristics.

The new company spent a few million dollars on cultural workshops like "Sexual Harassment in the American Workplace" and "German Dining Etiquette." But those were superficial, too.

From Daimler employees' perspective, the goal of automaking was uncompromising beauty and precision. "Quality at all cost," they would say. But to Chrysler workers, the goal was utility and affordability for their customers.

The Americans thought their new German coworkers were elitist. The Germans thought the Americans were risk takers with bad taste. Some Daimler executives even told the press that they "would never drive a Chrysler."

Though their complexions were similar, DaimlerChrysler employees were as different as can be.

Less than ten years later, the two companies broke up. Schrempp left amid shareholder anger. Eaton had been long gone by then. A private equity firm paid a reported $6 billion—10 percent of Chrysler's 1998 value—to spin the Americans out. Soon after, that company went bankrupt.

Aside from the massive price tag attached, this is not a rare story in the business world. More than half of mergers lose value rather than maintain it. Half of those say the most significant factor in the failure was "organizational cultural differences." Thirty-three percent say "cultural integration issues."

In other words, most mergers that lose money don't do so because of bad business. They lose money because their people can't deal with their differences.

It doesn't take a whole merger for this to happen, either. The same thing occurs when companies simply hire people from different demographic backgrounds and merge them into their workforces. At the time of this writing, 90 percent of Fortune 500 companies had hired a head "diversity officer" of some sort to help recruit and keep demographically diverse employees, because teams made of people of different races and genders and ages, they argue, would be smarter—much like what I argued in the last chapter. But like mergers, hiring statistics show something disheartening. Adding people who are different to the team usually causes problems.

The research is straightforward. Racial, cultural, and gender "diversity tends to lead to increased conflict," conclude professors from four universities in a sweeping study for the *Strategic Management Journal*. Adds Dr. Nigel Bassett-Jones of Oxford Brookes University, "Heterogeneous groups experience more conflict, higher turnover, less social integration and more problems with communication."

This puts organizations in a pickle. "If they embrace [demographic] diversity, they risk workplace conflict," Dr. Bassett-Jones writes. "And if they avoid diversity, they risk loss of competitiveness."

Welcome to the paradox of differences.

As we learned in our exploration of law enforcement and the parable of Problem Mountain, cognitive diversity makes us smarter. But unfortunately, all the studies show, it also makes us more conflict prone. And that conflict often blows our teams up before we can make use of our differences.

A review of seven hundred US companies by Harvard professors concluded that not only did most demographic diversity programs have no positive effect, but many made things worse for minorities. Research on government diversity hiring programs found no evidence that they "created a more equitable work environment for women or people of color." Zero. And more disheartening, research from Portland State University found that assigning only minorities to run "diversity management" programs "further marginalizes these already marginalized groups." It actually deepens the divisions.

On a civic level, a study by the Harvard political scientist Robert Putnam shows us that the greater a town's or country's ethnic diversity, the fewer people voted or volunteered. As we mentioned in the last chapter, diverse cities tend to produce more inventions and patents. But Putnam's research showed that they also had lower social trust—meaning people were more nervous around their neighbors. And follow-on research shows that this social trust is a more powerful predictor of economic growth than "levels of human capital or skills."

Ahhhhhhhhh!

But wait. Didn't we spend the last chapter talking about how differences are what *give* us progress? Didn't we learn that companies with diverse leadership make more profits? Didn't we discover that police departments and intelligence agencies get better when they include women and other different kinds of people?

Get ready to be depressed. Despite everything we learned in the last chapter, a study of 464 police departments across America found that the departments with the most racial diversity had the most officers who were fired or quit. Studies show the same is true of most businesses in general. Sure, differences lead to problem solving, but they also tend to lead to conflict among collaborators.

Imagine, for a moment, that you are Chris Jung in the early 1970s. You're starting your first job after graduating from the FBI Academy. You show up to your office and find that you are the only woman. You're also the only agent of Asian descent. The male agents all get along extremely well. They go for beers together every other Friday. They talk in sports metaphors and have their own "bro" code. When you speak and act a little differently than the gang, some of them are annoyed. When you suggest a wine bar for Friday's drinks one week instead of the sports bar, they laugh at the idea. When you get ignored or interrupted in meetings, no one seems to notice but you. Perhaps you stand up for yourself, and they get irritated.

Worst of all, half of your colleagues don't even realize any of this is bothering you.

There's a reason we use the term "culture fit" so much at work.

It's because when we have it, we have peace. If you're the cultural outsider in a tight-knit team of coworkers, your unique ideas and perspectives are useful. But your presence causes some friction. If only you could be more like the rest of the gang.

And that's the upshot with DaimlerChrysler. If the newly merged company's employees hadn't had so much cognitive diversity, there would have been less conflict. And with less conflict, that merger wouldn't have lost so much money.

Or so they thought.

2.

A few years before Daimler and Chrysler joined forces, another merger was taking shape in the government housing projects of New York City—a merger that would change the life of Robert Fitzgerald Diggs.

Diggs had ten siblings and grew up in ten different projects. His last memory of his father was from when he was a toddler. It was of Dad smashing up furniture with a hammer, right before he left Mom.

Diggs's mother's meager wages kept the family in government-subsidized apartments. Queens, then Brooklyn, then Staten Island. In one basement-level room, Diggs and five brothers slept on two twin beds. Sometimes heavy rains would cause the sewer to back up and fill their window view.

He was a thoughtful kid. He would later write about the silver lining of that miserable life. "Living where shit floats was a source of precious wisdom," he observed.

Religion became his lifeline. First Baptist Bible study. Then Islam, with its lessons about mathematics and peace. Then Taoism. Ten-year-old Diggs decided he liked them all.

But he got swept up in street business anyway. Selling drugs, running around with gangs. At one point, a teenager shot and killed one of Diggs's friends. In the '80s neither Jesus nor Muhammad could keep kids in the projects out of "the life."

In his early twenties, Diggs moved to Cleveland. He immediately got caught in cross fire between rival gangs. One day when he was driving his cousin's girlfriend home, he was ambushed by jealous gang members. They shot at the car, the girl, and Diggs. Diggs returned fire. The car took a beating. A person took a bullet. And Diggs went to trial. The city wanted eight years for "attempted murder" because Diggs fired a pistol into the dark.

A black kid from the New York projects didn't stand a chance against a motivated Cleveland prosecutor looking to make an example of what happens to gangbangers who move to *his* town. But Diggs went to the law library. He studied day and night to prepare a statement for when he took the stand. When his turn came, he delivered an impassioned speech. He told his story.

The effect was so powerful that three of the eleven white jurors hugged Diggs after declaring him "not guilty." The headline in the local newspaper read something like, "Jury Cries as Diggs Sentence Comes."

It was a second chance. "I got eight years of my life back in my own hands," he said. He stopped smoking and drinking until he could take control again. He quit hanging out with gangs. He moved back to New York.

Growing up, Diggs had an eclectic assortment of hobbies. He could quote the plot of any kung fu film the local library had on order. And his second religion (after his homespun Christianislamotaoism) was chess. He and the other kids in the projects played for thousands of hours. And like his peers, Diggs was entranced by a new type of music emerging from the Bronx in the late '70s and early

'80s: hip-hop. He had started recording hip-hop beats on makeshift equipment at age eleven.

After the trial, Diggs began taking long, meditative walks.

On those walks he developed a vision. He would blend his favorite things—chess, kung fu, religion, and music—into one. "Meditation allowed me to connect them all, to see their possibilities," he later wrote. "I realized that nobody else could do that at the time, because nobody had that particular group of experiences." He would use them to start the greatest rap group ever. But it wouldn't be any rap group, he decided. It would be an empire. A rap *army*. And he would name it the Wu-Tang Clan, after his favorite kung fu movie, *Shaolin and Wu Tang*.

It was a ridiculous idea.

Thus begins our second merger. Diggs recruited the best amateur rappers he knew from the Brooklyn and Staten Island projects. They ended up with nine guys, including Diggs. A few of them he knew already: his cousins Gary and Russell, and his roommate Dennis. Most of the others were drug dealers, guys Diggs had met in the street business. Some were even from rival gangs. Diggs used their love of hip-hop plus the carrot of getting out of the projects to lure them together to hear his plan.

It was simple enough. "Give me five years, and I will make you number one." Diggs would create the beats, and each rapper would write his own lyrics. Each would create his own kung fu persona, and Diggs would decide who got to record what. Each man would pitch in a few bucks, and Diggs would produce their first single.

The nine men agreed and pooled whatever cash they had.

And so, in October 1992, Gary Grice (aka GZA), Russell Jones (Ol' Dirty Bastard aka ODB), Clifford Smith (Method Man), Corey Woods (Raekwon the Chef), Dennis Coles (Ghostface Killah), Jason Hunter (Inspectah Deck), Lamont Hawkins (U-God), Jamel Irief

(Masta Killa), and Robert Fitzgerald Diggs—who from then on became known as The RZA—booked a recording studio.

And then they nearly killed one another.

3.

On the surface, the members of Diggs's hip-hop crew were as similar as the respective engineers and managers at Daimler and Chrysler. They were all young black alpha males who'd grown up in the projects of New York City. They all loved their hip-hop craft, and each was more or less down with kung fu.

But that was about where the resemblances ended.

Some of the guys were from the Stapleton projects, others from Park Hill. A couple weren't even from Staten Island—they were from rival projects in Brooklyn. They made a big deal about this.

And egos aside, their personalities were far from similar. Some were calm, others violent. The oldest was twenty-six, while the youngest was pushing seventeen.

They loved hip-hop, but each of them had a different *style* of hip-hop. ODB was charismatic and rhythmically unpredictable. GZA and Masta Killa were cerebral and laid-back. Method Man had grit-voiced braggadocio. Raekwon rapped fast and aggressively, while Inspectah Deck waxed intricate. Ghostface's style was more emotional, while U-God's was blaxploitative.

Diggs thought these contrasts were cool. But nine cooks with different tastes was a recipe for food poisoning.

Like Daimler and Chrysler employees suddenly working together, social trust in the Wu-Tang Clan was low. RZA and Method Man, perhaps the two most talented artists in the group, argued like crazy. But no two trusted each other less than Raekwon and Ghostface. Rae thought Ghost was a "crook." They'd been enemies in the neighborhood for too long.

"We didn't know each other enough to really trust each other," Raekwon told me later, referring to the group as a whole. "Differences is differences, ya know?"

As the nine young men gathered to work on hip-hop, they immediately got in each other's faces. Some of them carried guns with them when they went out, which meant their constant bickering could easily turn to violence.

But Diggs managed to keep their guns in their pockets long enough to present part two of his plan.

"It was almost like he did a Gotti move," Raekwon recalled years later. "He brought all the families to the table." And then he did something clever.

Being in the crew didn't mean your voice was going to be on the record, RZA announced. He was going to produce Wu-Tang's tracks the way hip-hop itself was born in the underground party scene.

Every session was going to be a battle of lyrics, RZA told them. He'd make a beat, and they should come prepared to compete on the microphone.

After all, he said, "Hip-hop was a war."

4.

Andre: Hip-hop all started in Jamaica with DJ culture and sound system culture.

This is Andre Torres, the executive editor of Rap Genius. I was sitting with him in a converted warehouse in Gowanus, Brooklyn, trying to bone up on my hip-hop history. Having grown up on

*pop-punk and country music in the middle of farm territory, I
didn't even know how to pronounce "RZA" (it's "Rizza") when I
first started lining up interviews with Wu-Tang and other rappers.*

Andre: It eventually made its way, with Kool Herc, to the Bronx
because he was Jamaican. They would have sound clashes. You
know, one sound system DJ battling another.

Shane: They were playing at the same time?

Andre: Yeah.

Shane: So, these battles . . . were two disc jockeys trying to get
people to come over and dance on their side of the party?

Andre: Yeah, to a point where you were going to drown the other
guy out.

Rob: Sorry I'm late. Came all the way from Staten Island.

This is Rob Markman, Rap Genius artist relations.

Shane: No problem. We were talking about how hip-hop developed.

Andre: I was getting into . . . this tension that started literally with
the DJs and sound systems. It wasn't about the MC—

(Master of Ceremonies)

—It was all about the DJ. The MC really was in support. He was
there to just "big up" the DJ.

Shane: Sort of the like the hype man.

Rob: That's what it was. The first MCs, they weren't even talking
about how good they were. It was like, "How good my DJ is."

Then when another DJ came on the set, *his* MC would talk about
how good *his* DJ is. Eventually it started competitions. The MCs
would take different shots at each other.

Andre: One of the turning points was the Busy Bee vs. Kool Moe
D battle at . . . Harlem World?

Rob: Yeah, it was Harlem World.

Andre: In 1982. You can hear part of it online. That was a break from what started out as, you know, "Throw your hands in the air!" You know, the little short party couplets.

I listened to the clip. Busy Bee's hyping the crowd up by shouting things like, "Ba wit the ba yo bang da bang diggy diggy! Say ho! Come on y'all!"

Andre (cont'd): Busy Bee was the top dude. Kool Moe D was on the come-up with a group called Treacherous Three at the time. He was looking at Busy Bee like, "This dude ain't all that."
Then he comes up and just destroyed him with like five minutes of way beyond any just straight party. He was getting personal.

Kool Moe D: "Hold on, Busy Bee, I don't mean to be bold. But put that "ba–ditty–ba" bullshit on hold. We gonna get right down to the nitty-grit. Gonna tell you little somethin' why you ain't shit."

Andre (cont'd): That was a new way of doing this MC thing. It became more like, "Oh, I'm going to come up and I'm going to crush you and make you look like a fool."

Rob: It was a crowd-pleaser because it was like nothing you ever heard.

Andre: They were loving it.

Rob: Busy Bee at the time—Busy Bee is the man. He's part of the reason that you come to the party in the first place. You know how they always say most people watch a Floyd Mayweather fight to see him lose? It wasn't that you came to see Busy Bee lose, but when he got taken out, it was just a new twist. That's when it started shifting.

Andre: Yeah!

Rob: These battles became legendary. You would tape the live performance and people would pass those around and treat those like records.

Andre: Eventually when these recordings make it to record, it sort
   of sets the standard.
Shane: So that idea of the battle basically created hip-hop?
Andre: Without a doubt.
Rob: They had a song literally called "Meth vs. Chef." RZA made
   them battle for it.
Andre: Which, I think, forced the creativity.

5.

In their efforts to win over partygoers, 1970s Bronx DJs and their
hype men didn't only give birth to a new genre, they created a
laboratory for musical innovation. Week after week, competing musicians would write new lyrics in preparation for the next battle. "If
you got beaten, then you couldn't wait till the next Friday to try
again," hip-hop historian and author Jeff Chang told me. You came
back to the party with something fresh.

The musicians often found their advantage by hacking their
sound equipment itself. There was no such thing as a "fader" switch
to allow you to turn the volume down on a speaker while still listen-
ing to it in headphones. A DJ named Grandmaster Flash soldered
such a switch onto his gear, allowing him to mix and match pieces
of two different records back and forth like it was magic. This is a
staple of any kind of DJ performance today but at the time was
groundbreaking. When electronic sound machines came out, DJs
broke them open to add computer memory. This let them play "sam-
ples," or snippets from other songs, or even violin or drums by pressing keys.

Battling pushed musicians to be more inventive, and to combine
diverse ideas into new sounds. Even though on the surface the hip-

hop battles were often competitions between individuals, the competitors became a sort of team that pushed the genre forward. Out of their battles sprang not just hip-hop, but R&B, techno, electronica, and whatever the hell dubstep is.

Diggs paid for the studio time to record the Wu-Tang Clan's first single in quarters.

There, he channeled his rappers' diverse aggressions into the microphone. Each member dug deep and showed up to record as if for a real battle. "Wu-Tang Clan truly did take a martial arts approach," Diggs later wrote, "to the sound of the music, the style of the lyrics, the competitive wordplay of the rhyming, the mental preparations involved." They made a single called "Protect Ya Neck"—with eight rappers and seven verses—and started selling it out of the trunk of a car.

The sound wasn't just unique. It was epic.

A few months went by, and then a DJ on a local New York radio station played the track. The Wu-Tang couldn't believe it. High off that momentum, they holed up in a basement on Morningstar Road to record a full-length album: *Enter the Wu-Tang: 36 Chambers.*

Diggs siphoned electricity from the neighbors to run his borrowed equipment: an eight-track, a sampler, and a keyboard. He cribbed drumbeats from old soul albums and sound effects from the film *Shaolin and Wu Tang.*

Diggs didn't come out of the basement for months. His eyes grew sunken. His Afro grew nappy (his words). Ghostface shoplifted canned food from the local grocery to feed him.

Finally, The RZA took off his headphones and played the record.

36 Chambers was a masterpiece. Their combined musicianship had created a sound no one on planet Earth had ever heard.

It would take three years of playing underwhelming clubs and selling records out of trunks for the world to finally notice. But when it did, *36 Chambers* went platinum. Wu-Tang Clan's second album would debut at number one on Billboard. Its members would go on to collectively sell seventy-four million records over the next twenty years. They would inspire a host of future Grammy winners—from Kanye West to Kendrick Lamar to white boys like Macklemore and Ryan Lewis.

Critics from *Rolling Stone* to the *Village Voice* would eventually call them the greatest rap group of all time.

6.

Our two stories present us with another paradox. Both in the case of DaimlerChrysler and in the case of the Wu-Tang Clan, teams which at first appeared similar were in fact hiding fundamental areas of difference. Cognitive diversity led these apparently homogenous groups into big conflict. In one case, that conflict destroyed a company. In the other case, it changed music history.

As we can see, it would be too hasty of us to repeat the myth that "the conflict that arises from our differences is bad."

But it would be equally hasty to generalize the opposite.

Conflict in the hip-hop industry was often far from productive. Things got ugly in the rap scene. The first hip-hop pioneers were competing only for a crowd in a dance hall. But in the late 1990s, the war came to be centered on issues of money and "turf."* East Coast rappers developed beef with West Coast rappers, and vice

---

*Shockingly, in Idaho, I was oblivious to this whole war until a decade later.

versa. Instead of challenging each other musically, some artists started challenging each other with guns.

Things came to a head when two rival rappers were assassinated in close succession.

"The big moment of truth was after Tupac was murdered and after Biggie was murdered," Chang, the hip-hop historian, explains. "This massive evolution of style occurred because of the battle. But then the battle spilled into the streets. Conflict helped the industry innovate, but at what point does conflict become counterproductive?"

To get at the answer, we're going to go back in time.

The year is 1901. It's a sunny summer day, and you're walking down Third Street in Dayton, Ohio. Two-story brick buildings line the road. Small storefronts, manufacturing shops, ice cream parlors. Birds are chirping, pedestrians are chatting. It's an idyllic Midwestern scene.

As you stroll past the striped awning of a bicycle shop, you hear a jarring sound coming from inside. Shouting.

If you were to walk by this same bicycle shop again, you'd learn that the shouting went on every day. It commenced in the morning, paused around noon, and resumed after lunch.

This nonstop ruckus was commonplace at the company's previous location on South Williams Street, and it carried on unabated at the company's next shop in North Carolina.

But the fighting was not, as it might appear, a symptom of an abusive relationship. It was simply the way these two shopkeepers worked.

When they needed to solve a problem, they would raise their voices and start arguing. But then the shopkeepers would do something interesting. After a fair amount of debate, they would stop, switch sides of the argument, and start yelling again. The one who'd just debated *against* something would now argue *for* it, and vice versa. They'd do this until they worked out a solution to whatever they were stuck on.

For most of us, schizophrenic yelling matches may sound like a hostile work environment.

But most of us aren't Wilbur and Orville Wright, the inventors of human flight.

As a kid, I discovered a great way to irritate my own brother: shooting him with a makeshift rubber-band gun comprising my forefinger and thumb. In physics, there's a concept called "potential energy" that's illustrated well by this brotherly attack. A regular old rubber band lying on a table has very little potential energy. If you leave it alone, it's not going to do anything. But when you pull the rubber band from two directions and stretch it, suddenly it has a *lot* of potential energy. If you let go of it, it will go flying.

And the more you stretch the rubber band—or put another way, the more tension you put on it—the more potential energy the rubber band has. The farther you can shoot it.

Of course, at a certain point if you stretch the rubber band too much, it will snap. All that potential energy breaks the rubber band, and now it's inert again. We might chart the rubber band's potential like this:

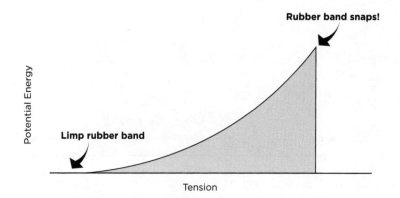

We can use rubber-band physics as an analogy for potential energy in a relationship between a group of people. Whenever different ways of thinking collide, they create tension. A cognitively diverse team is like a group of people pulling on different sides of a rubber band. The more tension, the farther the rubber band can launch if it's pointed in the right direction. Psychologists call this cognitive friction—where cognitive diversity collides and creates potential energy.

Just like a rubber band, if the tension in a group of different people gets too great, things break down. The group snaps. It makes no progress.

At the other end of the spectrum—in the absence of tension— there's also no progress. A group of people standing around like a limp rubber band goes nowhere.

Between these two extremes—between inertia and destruction— lies a zone of possibility. This is where the magic of group progress happens. We might call this area where cognitive friction creates potential energy the Tension Zone. But to simplify, and because Tension Zone sounds like a Kenny Loggins song from the 1980s, let's just refer to it as The Zone.

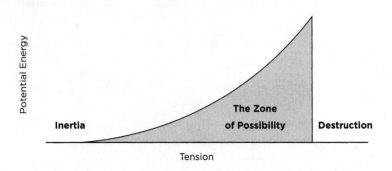

In American slang, "being in the zone" implies that a person is focused and able to perform their best at something. So it's not inappropriate for us to say that The Zone, in capital letters, is where that kind of magic happens for a team. And the important ingredient, the thing that gets teams into The Zone, is not peace and harmony and sameness—it's engaging the tension between their perspectives, heuristics, ideas, and differences.

When we look at the history of great collaborations, we see this pattern everywhere. In fact, *every* successful cognitively diverse relationship takes place inside The Zone. And it's the key to explaining our merger paradox.

At one point when they were working on their airplane, Orville and Wilbur Wright had a problem with the propeller. They needed something to propel the vehicle forward, which a spinning blade could in theory accomplish, but it was unclear how to make it work, to get the plane off the ground without sending it out of control. So, as usual, the arguments began.

They shouted back and forth at each other for weeks. They flip-flopped sides of the arguments, and eventually realized that they were both wrong. The solution wasn't a propeller; it was two propellers, each spinning a different direction. Which is just about the perfect meta-analogy for how The Zone works.

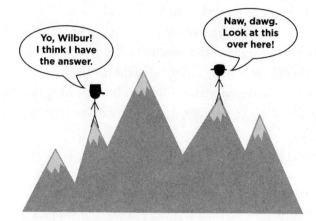

Orville and Wilbur knew that neither was going to think up the design of an airplane by himself. Their arguments created tension that pushed them into The Zone where progress was possible.

But while arguing helped the brothers explore new intellectual territory together, it also created the danger of going too far—of devolving into real fights, or hurt feelings, like a rubber band ready to snap.

So, to keep the tension safely within The Zone, Wilbur and Orville did their little debate switcheroo. This technique helped them to decouple the arguments from their personal egos, which in turn helped them look at things from different perspectives without getting too mad. It depersonalized the conflict, ensuring that the goal was always to make progress up the mountain rather than to kill each other.

"I don't think they really got mad," said a mechanic who worked with them. "But they sure got awfully hot."

In his basement studio, Robert Diggs harnessed the cognitive friction between his rappers' diverse styles and personalities—and also the tension between his own diverse tastes—to create a new sound. By channeling the potential energy from the Clan's rap battles into a collective goal, Diggs was able to make the hip-hop world's most powerful rubber-band gun, so to speak. He managed to keep things inside The Zone long enough to make Wu-Tang superstars.*

Diggs's strategy of scrambling different rap styles together spilled into each individual rapper's technique. Raekwon shared his experience of street life through culinary metaphors. Method Man mingled drug references with *Green Eggs & Ham* and classic Dick Van Dyke songs. Inspectah Deck reflected on gang violence, Greek philosophy, and science.

At times, though, the conflict at Wu-Tang went too far. Over the years, the group fought and sparred and walked out on one another dozens and dozens of times. In 1997, as Chrysler and Daimler were crafting their merger plan, persistent infighting forced Wu-Tang to drop out of its massive tour with rock band Rage Against the Machine.

---

*And as they battled, something happened to each of the rappers individually. The tension between their diverse ways of thinking helped them broaden their own perspectives and heuristics. Each artist began to develop curiosity and respect for other styles, which helped each to become a more fluent and diverse thinker himself.

Which reminds me. What about our poor friends at DaimlerChrysler? Their relationship wasn't nearly as volatile as Wu-Tang's. The Germans and the Americans were different, sure, but they never got in any shouting matches.

It turns out their problem wasn't too much conflict at all. It was the exact opposite.

7.

Any science writer who ends up writing about relationships eventually ends up at the Gottman Institute. I was no exception to the cliché when I started digging into the science of Dream Teams.

At their research center in Seattle, Drs. John Gottman and Julie Schwartz Gottman study romantic partnerships and what makes them tick. I found them because of my interest in what makes lovers *stop* ticking. What causes partners who once thought that they'd be better together to call it quits?

The answer is surprising, but quite simple.

"Interaction patterns, such as disagreement and anger exchanges," they report, "may not be harmful in the long run." In fact, conflicts can be "predictive of improvement" in partnership satisfaction over time.

The reason is not because arguing makes us happy. It's actually because if you're still arguing, you're probably still together. There's potential energy in the rubber band you're stretching together. If you keep talking long enough—and those arguments don't spill over into violence—you're going to eventually work things out.

Indeed, the biggest leading indicator that a marriage is about to end is not, in fact, when couples argue. It's when they *stop* talking.

Two experiments help us connect this to our exploration of differences and teamwork. First, a group of researchers from Harvard, Berkeley, and the University of Minnesota decided that they wanted to know just how much training people to be mindful of demographic diversity helped big companies with lots of employees. So they found 829 businesses that emphasized diversity training and tracked how they fared over a period of thirty-one years. In 2007 they published their surprising results. That is, that so-called diversity training programs had "no positive effects in the average workplace." In fact, they found "in firms where training is mandatory or emphasizes the threat of lawsuits, training actually has negative effects." Emphasizing how not to offend people who were different scared employees into disengaging.

Then in a 2015 experiment, another group of professors took a group of white men who were applying for an IT job, and separated them into two groups. Before the job interview, they told half of the men about the great efforts the company they were applying to used to focus on racial diversity. The other half weren't told anything about that. The job applicants who'd gotten the diversity message did worse in their job interviews. Their heart rates rose. They were more nervous. They talked less. Talking about race differences made them freeze up.

And this was, according to the professors, "regardless of these men's political ideology, attitudes toward minority groups, beliefs about the prevalence of discrimination against whites, or beliefs about the fairness of the world."* †

These two experiments reveal something about human nature. Our most primal reaction when we are put together with people who

---

*They go on to say: "This suggests just how widespread negative responses to diversity may be . . . the responses exist even among those who endorse the tenets of diversity and inclusion."

†Note how the imprecise language in all of these studies conflates racial diversity with the catchall term "diversity" itself. Someone please go yell at them!

aren't like us is precisely the reaction of these test subjects. We tend to freeze. We get nervous about the tension we see coming, so we clam up. Even if we have good intentions toward other people.

A managing director who oversaw demographic diversity at one of the world's largest banks put it well to me one night over dinner. "One of the biggest problems we have is we hire all these different kinds of people and then tell them to fit our way of thinking," she told me. She would soon leave her job to oversee diversity at the world's other largest bank, where the same thing would happen. "They have all this potential to add to the culture," she said. "And you watch them slowly learn to keep quiet." If you're different from other people in your group, it's incredibly easy, and incredibly common, to get nervous and stop speaking up.

I tried to confirm this phenomenon myself. In 2016, I conducted a nationwide survey of employees of a hundred major US corporations. I asked these employees about the differences between themselves and their coworkers and managers—whether they were in the minority or majority in various categories like race, gender, age, experience, education, and geographic background—and then asked various questions aimed at discerning how much they were able to use their different ways of thinking at work. I then cross-referenced this with data on how innovative their companies were. The upshot of the study shouldn't surprise us, given what we've been talking about. Businesses that rank high in "innovation"—the ones that grow quickly and produce game-changing products and services— tend to encourage the airing and clashing of diverse viewpoints. Not just having differences, but speaking up.

The data were persuasive. No matter how demographically diverse, organizations that let their people *use* their different mental tool kits are going to be more effective at finding new peaks on Problem Mountain. Companies that don't innovate tend to make people follow a single, "approved" way of thinking. Their different

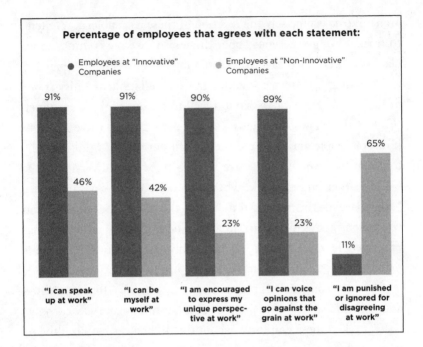

Percentage of employees that agrees with each statement:

● Employees at "Innovative" Companies   ● Employees at "Non-Innovative" Companies

| 91% | 91% | 90% | 89% | 65% |
| 46% | 42% | 23% | 23% | 11% |

"I can speak up at work" | "I can be myself at work" | "I am encouraged to express my unique perspective at work" | "I can voice opinions that go against the grain at work" | "I am punished or ignored for disagreeing at work"

kinds of people keep quiet about their different perspectives and heuristics. They break less ground than companies that encourage everyone to speak out.

And this, it turns out, was the festering sickness hidden in all those failed mergers we talked about.

In 2011, a group of professors from the University of Athens decided that they wanted to see exactly how people behave after their companies go through a merger. So they found some companies that were merging, met their employees, and put tracking devices on them.

They then sat back and observed where the people went, whom they interacted with, and what they said to one another. Numerous studies already supported the theory that integrating cultures was the most difficult part of a merger. But this was the first time anyone had looked at how much people from different companies actually *spoke* to one another.

The answer, it turned out, was not much. The professors observed that most mergers did not lead to an increase in fighting, but instead they led to an increase in something they called "organizational silence." Basically, this is when team members don't talk about important issues, or at all. Companies that had organizational silence developed a lack of social trust among their employees. And this led to mergers failing to live up to their potential.

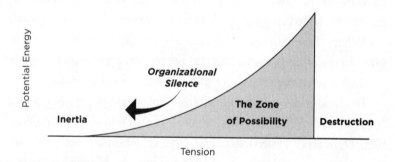

Rather than deal with the discomfort of cognitive friction that comes with everyone's different perspectives and heuristics, the people inside of most newly merged companies get quiet.* † And that, it turns out, is worse for business than arguing.

Organizational silence has contributed to some of the most spec-

---

*We wouldn't be crazy to suspect that this is the very reason that those demographically diverse cities we talked about earlier have lower levels of civic engagement.

†We'll dig deeper into what leads to this organizational silence in the next chapter!

tacular mistakes in history. After the infamous Bay of Pigs fiasco—one of the biggest US foreign policy blunders of the twentieth century—several former cabinet members would later admit they regretted not speaking up. President John F. Kennedy's team stood tacitly by while a gung-ho CIA persuaded the president to secretly land troops in Cuba. "In the months after the Bay of Pigs," Kennedy aide Arthur Schlesinger wrote, "I bitterly reproached myself for having kept so silent during those crucial discussions, though my feelings of guilt were tempered by the knowledge that a course of objection would have accomplished little save to gain me a name as a nuisance."

Imagine that once again you're the Chris Jung of your team, the person who thinks differently among a group of similar thinkers. How much time does it take before you start holding your tongue rather than keep bringing up ideas that create conflict for the group?

Where there's difference, there's tension. And where there's tension, there's often fear. And fearful people often avoid speaking up.

This is what the employees of Chrysler and Daimler did.

In the beginning, the Germans were afraid of coming across "heavy-handed." So they "stayed away from Detroit." Fearing conflict, DaimlerChrysler executives were reluctant to mesh the two organizations too closely—not even the brands. Married on paper,

* crickets chirping *

Mercedes, Dodge, Jeep, and the rest were strangers to one another. "Schrempp . . . told himself there is no point in trying to smash these two companies together," said Chrysler's former vice chairman.

Chrysler's chief, Bob Eaton, seemed withdrawn. He went weeks at a time without speaking to the head of Daimler. Whereas Eaton had once been fond of preaching what he called "participatory management," now he seemed like he'd stopped participating altogether.

Peter Stallkamp, one of the Chrysler executives responsible for the company's success in the '90s before the merger, told CNBC, "The managers feared for their careers, and in the absence of assurance, they assumed the worst. There were a good eighteen months when we were being hollowed out from the core by the Germans' inaction and our own paralysis."

Could we really have expected this to go well?

Within a couple of years, two crucial Chrysler VPs had packed up and left for jobs at Ford. A heavy cloud hung over the organization. Managers weren't engaged, employees weren't engaged. All the predicted "synergy" went out the window. Things began to fall apart at DaimlerChrysler. "What happened to the dynamic, can-do cowboy culture I bought?" Jürgen Schrempp lamented.

Most of the cowboys were still there. They'd just checked out of the rodeo.

8.

If any member of the Red Army hockey dynasty can be called a "secret ingredient," I'd argue that it's longtime team captain Valery Vasiliev. And not for the reasons one might initially assume.

You may recall that this was the guy who had a heart attack during a game and kept playing. Vasiliev was a hard worker, the embodiment of the cliché "leaving it all on the rink."

Compared to his teammates, Vasiliev could barely skate. He never scored. But his team didn't care. Because when Vasiliev was around, they did better.

This was due, in large part, to the role Vasiliev played in sparring with their coach. Coach Tikhonov, for all his rigor and discipline, was a tyrant. He would deny the players access to their families during practice season and wouldn't allow them to go to the funerals of loved ones. He would berate and pummel and abuse the players when they screwed up—and Vasiliev would fight back on their behalf, berating the coach when he made mistakes, too.

Fascinatingly, neither man seemed to take this stuff personally. Vasiliev would show up to practice the day after a physical fight with Tikhonov and act like nothing had happened. When Tikhonov pulled the good players and made the team lose the Miracle on Ice game in the Olympics, Vasiliev allegedly *choked* Tikhonov on the bus.

"Tikhonov knew Vasiliev would push back, do what these great captains do," says *Wall Street Journal* sports journalist and author Sam Walker. It was part of the process. "It wasn't a personal thing; it was about the team."

The Red Army didn't just benefit from the cognitive friction of its coaches' diverse stylistic inputs—the dance and ninja training, the marathon skating drills. They also benefited from the constant tension between coach and captain in the name of bettering the team.

Keith Yamashita, the founder of SYPartners and coach to Oprah and Steve Jobs whom we met earlier, likes to talk about how "microactions add up." A hundred small instances of being included as part of the group can lead to organizational trust, and even explain how people like Tikhonov and Vasiliev could fight like they did and still work together. They never stopped engaging each other in the name of the cause. On the other hand, a hundred small occasions of being ignored or excluded—even if each occasion on its own is innocent or not a big deal—leads us to feel like outsiders, perhaps even hated.* The team member who sits on the bench, doesn't get the high five, doesn't get asked for input, may as well be a ghost.

This is why research by Gallup shows that when a manager ignores his or her people, the chances of those people being "actively disengaged" are a whopping 40 percent. And, as writes Gallup's Tom Rath in his book *StrengthsFinder 2.0*, "Having a manager who ignores you is even more detrimental than having a manager who primarily focuses on your weaknesses."

The Red Army didn't have that problem. And neither did Wu-Tang.

In terms of self-destructive potential, Wu-Tang's merger of nine volatile personalities far outstripped DaimlerChrysler's "merger of equals." And yet despite the arguments, despite walking out on shows, despite some very public brawls over money, Wu-Tang managed to produce seven albums together over twenty-five years. There was no organizational silence. They were the family that never truly fell apart, because they kept coming back to hash things out.†

And as uncomfortable as the infighting was, Diggs recognized that it was this very friction that made them powerful.

"When steel rubs against steel," RZA said, "it makes both blades sharper."

---

*Present-day parlance calls these "microaggressions." An individual slight may not be a big deal, but if you happen to be the one thousandth person to deliver said slight, you might make someone feel much worse than you assume they would, or should. It's hard for me not to get angry at the fiftieth person who calls me "Shawn" instead of Shane. And so many microaggressions people endure every day are so much worse than that!

†Besides, as Amos Barshad pointed out in *Grantland*, "They climbed out of the slums of Shaolin. It was never gonna be pretty."

9.

The 1983 movie *Shaolin and Wu Tang* opens with a dojo scene. Students from two rival schools are tussling. One school is Shaolin, which specializes in a secret fist technique. The other is Wu Tang: keepers of a secret sword strategy.

Both teachers throw in the towel early. "Don't show him too much!" the Shaolin master warns. The elders are less afraid of losing than they are of the kids giving away their secrets.

Before long, the bad guy, the evil Qing Lord, learns about the schools' secret techniques through his spies. Realizing that they pose a threat to his power, the Qing Lord hatches a plan to eliminate them. He holds a martial arts contest, hoping that each dojo will destroy the other.

But the two rival kids from Act 1 get wind of what the Qing Lord is up to. They join forces. When they combine their unique heuristics—the Shaolin fist and the Wu Tang sword—they create a deadly combination. The Qing Lord is appropriately defeated.

"You're genius to have mixed the two!" the empress tells the young warriors in the final scene.

Robert Diggs didn't just mix two techniques. He mixed nine of them. And in kung fu tradition, each of his nine master rappers mixed various styles, foreign ideas, and nonmusical metaphors into his own musical process.

A decade after bringing the Wu-Tang Clan together, Diggs could finally afford to travel the seven thousand miles that lie between New York City and the real Shaolin. He could finally afford to see the real Wu Tang Mountain.

"When we stood on this mountain and looked up at the range of peaks called the Nine Dragons, this is what we saw," he recalled. "Three mountains forming a giant 'W'—the symbol I chose to represent a crew of nine men, nine years earlier. It was as plain as day, and has been for a million years. But some things aren't visible until you're truly ready to see them."

Diggs's obsessions gave him a unique set of perspectives when he looked at his own mountain—the mountain he and his brothers would have to climb if they were ever going to get out of the projects.

Kung fu taught Diggs that friction sharpens our mental weapons, and that those weapons are more powerful together than alone. Spiritual mathematics had taught him that seemingly conflicting things can combine to form something wonderful. And chess taught him, like Valery Vasiliev and the Wright brothers, to depersonalize conflict in the name of getting better.

"The most important thing is to realize that the problem is on the board," Diggs would reminisce. "It's not with you."

As we can see, there's enormous potential energy in diverse perspectives and heuristics. But we can't unlock that energy unless we knock our heads together. Dream Teams, in other words, predictably require tension.

It's a compelling idea—the power of The Zone. But as Diggs learned, as Daimler learned, as the Wright Brothers learned, making our cognitive diversity work for us isn't easy. So often, the same tension that can lead to progress instead leads to destruction or inertia because we can't handle our differences.

The problem—and, as I would soon discover, also the solution— lies in a tiny cluster of cells at the center of our brains.

שְׁלוֹשָׁה

——⊙⊙——

THE MAGIC CIRCLE

"These rats are depressed."

1.

The mood in Buenos Aires at the turn of the twentieth century—for its immigrant residents, at least—was tense.

Nestled along the beautiful Rio de la Plata on the southeast coast of South America, the capital of Argentina grew from two hundred thousand people to 1.5 million between 1870 and 1910. Most of these newcomers were not Argentinian babies. They were Italians, Germans, Hungarians, Russians, and natives of a hundred other places.

When it became an independent nation in the mid-1800s, Argentina had the same landmass as Europe, but one-fifth the population of London. The government wanted immigrants. Immigrants to develop the land, immigrants to build the economy and pay taxes. So in the late 1800s officials distributed 130,000 free tickets for Europeans to cross the Atlantic and settle. Those who sailed sent back word about how great Argentina was. And the ships kept coming.

Buenos Aires ballooned into a thriving, dirty metropolis. Like other immigrant-heavy cities such as New York and São Paulo, each wave of newcomers added to the urban friction. Immigrants proudly spoke their native languages in defiance of the local Spanish. Skirmishes between various ethnic groups erupted. And with each new group in each new place came the fear that an old group's way of life would crumble.

Such was the case in Buenos Aires when the first Jewish families arrived.

The Argentines weren't thrilled about non-Christians moving in. They didn't understand how Jewish people did things or why. And the government didn't like the idea of Jewish people owning land. Jewish families had left homes and livelihoods in Eastern Europe in the hope of a better future. Inevitably, however, they found themselves pushed into the less-desirable parts of Buenos Aires. By 1910, there were sixty-eight thousand Jewish people living in the city.

You can sense the locals' fear in the newspaper headlines of the day. "Are We Becoming A Semitic Republic?" asked an article in 1898 in the *Buenos Aires Herald*. "The immigration of Russian Jews is now the third largest in the list, while Syrian Arabs (Turks) and Arabians are also flocking to these shores."

Jewish people were effectively barred from good neighborhoods and civic participation. They were victims of hate speech and, occasionally, violence.

Many locals heightened the tension by championing the myth of the "true Argentino": *el gaucho*. Gauchos were portrayed as macho, patriotic, horse-riding cowboys who stood for everything you had to be to fit in in Argentina. The gaucho was a South American Marlboro Man—born and bred on the pampas. You weren't a real Argentino, people said, if you didn't have a little gaucho in you.

No strangers to persecution, Argentinian Jews faced a wrenching choice: either lose their identity and conform to this culture, or lose their shot at a persecution-free life. The gaucho thing just didn't work for most of them. *Will we get driven out of here, too?* they wondered.

So far in *Dream Teams*, we've seen that extraordinary collaborations are powered by differences, and that breakthrough progress is the product of cognitive friction. But as we talked about in the last chapter, groups often fail to reach their potential because friction tends to make people nervous. In this chapter, I want to dig into how we can reduce the fear that prevents us from getting together and doing the work we are meant to do. How do we move high-potential, but overly tense relationships back into The Zone, where magic can happen?

The Wright brothers' debate-and-switch tactic was a great way for the two of them to keep their conflict constructive. Changing sides of their arguments prevented things from getting so personal that they might destroy each other. But this technique doesn't really apply in a situation like, say, trying to make 1920s Buenos Aires a good place to live for fearful locals and struggling immigrants. And having grown up in some of the roughest neighborhoods of New York City, the members of the Wu-Tang Clan were pretty good at facing down conflict, and thus were willing to come to RZA's battles to make records together. But the Jewish and Arab immigrants of Buenos Aires were not exactly lining up to have stirring debates about community projects with the gauchos. And so, what happened in their city is what happened in most immigrant cities: people became more or less segregated into parts of the city where they could have minimal interaction with people not like them.

Operating a city—or any size community for that matter—takes a lot of teamwork. Economies grow when people interact. Streets stay safe and clean when everybody pitches in. Ensuring people have resources, protection, and stability isn't just the mayor's job.

This kind of social cooperation is the reason humans developed collaborative abilities in the first place. If you remember, we mentioned earlier that our brain's ability to interpret body language and facial expressions, and even language itself, is all part of an evolutionary tool kit that made *Homo sapiens* the dominant species on the planet. Thus puny, cooperative humans hunted woolly mammoths and giant armadillos to extinction. We figured out how to defend ourselves from predators, even kill them off.

And in a world without saber-toothed tigers, humans' biggest threat soon became *other* groups of humans.

At that point, ironically, the same survival instinct that pushed us to work together also pushed us to be jerks to people who weren't like us. Whereas we could generally trust our own tribespeople not to murder us in our sleep for a woolly mammoth steak, we came to count on neighboring tribes to want to do just that. Our brains developed a predisposition to view people who don't look or talk or act like us as potential threats.

Scientists call this *in-group psychology*. To speed up how fast we react to potential threats, a healthy human brain automatically tends to put people into one of two categories: the "safe" *in-group* (our tribe, or people with familiar attributes who we're naturally inclined to help and trust) and the "suspicious" *out-group*—every other human being on the planet.

Neuroscientists have discovered that our brains actually are hardwired for this. The culprits are called the amygdalae. They're a pair of oval-shaped lumps in the very middle of our brains, responsible for helping us identify threats, and then firing up a series of automatic responses to get our bodies ready to fight or flee when danger comes.

Here's how it works: Say you're walking down the street, and a minivan swerves from its lane toward you. Your brain interprets this new, loud, fast-approaching object as a threat. So your amygdalae go on alert. They trigger a waterfall of chemical responses. Your brain creates a molecule called glutamate that makes you freeze—or flinch—and pay attention. It then signals a part of the brain called the hypothalamus. The hypothalamus tells your glands to start pumping out adrenaline. This raises your heart rate and blood pressure, which gets you ready to either run or fight. (If you're smart, you don't fight in this particular case.)

Your brain is an amazing organ. In an instant you're ready to handle the threat.

This automatic fear response pays off in situations involving warring prehistoric tribes and out-of-control minivans. But it backfires when it comes to dealing with people in the modern world. Our amygdalae start the same chain reaction when we encounter people who don't look, speak, or act like we do, even if we're not in conflict.

The neurochemical sequence that goes off when we encounter something or someone foreign to us is hard to control. It creates tension with people who are different before we even have the chance to start working together. Left unchecked, our natural reaction to an out-group neighbor who moves to town is an impulse to avoid or to destroy.*†

The science is clear: if our amygdalae are normal, then we all have this "deep-rooted fear toward strangers or the unfamiliar." The Greek word for it is—get ready—"xenophobia."‡

---

*Daimler and Chrysler employees didn't want to fight, so they fled into organizational silence. Most of us aren't prepared to face Bob from Human Resources in deadly combat, regardless of how threatened we felt during our last performance review. So we avoid him.

†Research by neuro-economist Paul Zak shows that organizations with low trust have more people take sick days.

‡Typing the words "we all have xenophobia," by the way, is terrifying. In my journey to understand human collaboration, I had not expected to encounter scientific evidence that I was xenophobic. My initial reaction was to declare this bit of science wrong and delete the sentence. But then I realized that this very instinct proved the point. My response to a new, uncomfortable idea was to avoid it. So in the interest of not being a hypocrite, I kept the sentence. My consolation for my xenophobic brain is that yours is, too.

This got us pretty far because it was useful when the world was big enough for us to actually stay away from each other. But that was before we knew that a bad Starbucks is better than a good cave. The dawn of agriculture foretold that humans were going to be living at very close quarters.

At that point, the amygdalae and the in-group psychology that once helped us to survive stopped being as helpful. Not only are we now surrounded by our out-groups, but more than ever we need them and the cognitive diversity they bring in order to make progress.

Back in turn-of-the-century Buenos Aires, citizens began to panic when all the strange new people started flooding in.

On the one hand, the locals could ignore Jewish immigrants, relegating them to their own neighborhoods and leaving them out of civic matters. But what would happen if too many of them showed up? What if Jewish people decided *they* wanted the *intendente*'s office and a town house in the Recoleta? That was a war waiting to happen.

Another option, the locals' amygdalae surely suggested, was to oppress these immigrants. They could beat them down, deny them opportunities, maybe even kill them, as Adolf Hitler's regime would do not many years later in Europe.

The best choice, of course, would be to figure out how to trust each other. This would require doing one of two things. They could override the natural amygdalae process through sheer willpower—a difficult feat. Or they could figure out how to get all these foreign neighbors to become part of their in-group.

Of course in 1910 nobody was thinking about things in those terms.

In the history of the world only one nation—the United States—has taken in more immigrants than Argentina. In many ways the *Gangs of New York*–era tensions between immigrant groups in Manhattan were mirrored in Buenos Aires. The backlash against Jewish new-comers* threatened the city's stability—at first.

But then something wonderful happened. While Jewish people were persecuted and murdered in Europe, and relegated to segregated neighborhoods in New York, anti-Semitism in Buenos Aires plummeted. Buenos Aires became *the* place—outside of modern-day Israel—where Jewish people were most thoroughly accepted. Urban Argentina became renowned for its cosmopolitan culture. The Porteños'† fear of immigrants in general and their incidence of hate crime—targeting people for being different—dropped to among the lowest in the world. Argentines developed an identity that included immigrants on the team.

How did this happen? To find out, we're going to look at three stories about computer geeks.

---

*Virtually every immigrant group at the time faced some degree of marginalization. But in Buenos Aires (and in most other cities in the world at the time), Jewish immigrants got much of the worst of it.

†Residents of Buenos Aires call themselves Porteños—the people of the port.

2.

Our first group of computer geeks hailed from Massachusetts. It was 1999. As dust settled on the DaimlerChrysler merger, Carol Vallone, CEO of Universal Learning Technologies, was planning a buyout of her own.

ULT was well funded and growing fast. Its squad of computer programmers made tools for teachers to manage classes online. Meanwhile, in Vancouver, Canada, a professor at the University of British Columbia had been working on an online education company called WebCT. In two years, WebCT, a nonprofit, had signed up almost three million students.

It was the classic nonprofit-meets-for-profit romance. WebCT had connections and customers and loved walks in the rain. ULT had business and technology chops but was allergic to cats. Would they merge? Wouldn't they?

In the end Vallone got down on one knee. ULT bought out WebCT, and together they rode off into the digital sunset.

But honeymoons don't last forever. Vallone soon noticed how oppositional the cultures of her two offices were. One was a nonprofit on Canada's west coast, the other a for-profit on America's east coast. They had dramatically different points of view.

ULT's employees were ambitious and creative, almost to the point of impatience. They weren't thrilled when Vallone announced that they would take WebCT's name and adopt WebCT's platform.

WebCT's employees, on the other hand, were academic and cautious. "They felt like the Blue Suits were coming to Vancouver to take over the company," Vallone recalls. The conflict was obvious and immediate.

Organizational silence began to set in. The biggest fear on the

Canadian side, Vallone recalled, was that WebCT would now be focused on enriching its investors instead of building the industry. And the Americans feared that the Canadians' university and non-profit ethos would resist speed and innovation. Vallone worried whether the newlywed companies could really blend cultures. They were skeptical of each other. "How do we build trust?" Vallone asked.

The ULT-WebCT merger had all the potential for progress that diverse perspectives and heuristics bring. And it had all the potential for failure. "You're under attack," warned the employees' subconscious brains. "Time to run or fight!" Fear threatened to sink the whole enterprise.

3.

Computer geek story number two starts with a stereotype: "Nothing's scarier," said A. J. Harbinger, "than going up and talking to a beautiful woman."

I had once walked in on a full-grown bear eating all my food on a camping trip, so I begged to differ. But I kept that to myself.

We were in Los Angeles, at Harbinger's two-and-a-half-story man-pad. Here his company, Art of Charm, hosted a weeklong "confidence boot camp" for single men with social anxiety. I was working on a magazine story about it.

Harbinger's statement made me cringe at first. But then I considered his audience: eight terrified, nerdy* straight guys sitting on couches. One had a condition where his voice would squeak when

---

*You'll forgive me, but I know my own people.

he got nervous around people, which was always. Another was a shy Filipino immigrant who was petrified to talk to American women but really wanted to get married one day. Another was a computer programmer from Colorado who hadn't mustered the courage to ask someone on a date in years. Et cetera. Each man had his own slightly different story but was ultimately there because coed socialization scared him.

The first thing Harbinger did was bring in—get this—*an actual woman*! Her name was Suzanne. Our assignment was to take turns bantering with her in front of the group while Harbinger recorded it. Talking to strangers is my job, but in front of a confidence coach with a Flip camera, I felt suddenly intimidated. The geeks looked on in openmouthed wonder. My amygdalae started going nuts.

Each day the boot camp served up some version of this exercise. Monday it was Suzanne. Tuesday it was giving high fives to random strangers at a bar. Wednesday and Thursday it was playing silly games with a couple of ladies from a local improvisational comedy theater.

They made us pretend to be characters and act out skits with them—an ax murderer applying for a job, bodybuilders expressing effusive gratitude to each other, couples breaking up over ridiculous things, and so on. We formed circles and made up stories together where each person contributed one word at a time. We took turns rolling on the floor in laughter.

Harbinger called this "exposure therapy." The way to overcome the fear of a social situation, he said, was to put yourself in more of those situations. Afraid of strangers? Force yourself to meet some. Afraid of women? Force yourself to spend time with some.

Despite the apparent absurdity of some of the exercises, Harbinger cited a scientific rationale for this "therapy."

It's known as mere exposure effect, and it's based on classic research by social psychologist Robert Zajonc and illustrated well by the following newspaper report in 1967:

A mysterious student has been attending a class at Oregon State University for the past two months enveloped in a big black bag. Only his bare feet show. Each Monday, Wednesday, and Friday at 11:00 A.M. the Black Bag sits on a small table near the back of the classroom. The class is Speech 113—basic persuasion. . . . Charles Goetzinger, professor of the class, knows the identity of the person inside. None of the 20 students in the class do. Goetzinger said the students' attitude changed from hostility toward the Black Bag to curiosity and finally to friendship.

At first, the students in this college class were not especially nice to the strange, mute person in the black bag. But merely being exposed to it over and over led students to stop being afraid of it—even to like it! Zajonc used this and other studies to show how humans become less scared of things the more they encounter them.

At Art of Charm, repeatedly interacting with Suzanne and other strangers was like Harbinger's man-in-the-bag. Most of the guys had spent their lives avoiding interaction with unfamiliar people. Getting them to interact with strangers over and over was not only good practice but also psychological fear-busting.

By week's end I saw a dramatic difference in our little AV club. The geeks were walking up to strangers in bars, asking them to dance, striking up conversations on Hollywood Boulevard.

I was impressed. Harbinger's therapy was working!

It would be easy for us to conclude from Harbinger's geeks and the mere exposure theory that Buenos Aires got more tolerant toward Jewish people simply because they lived there. But that doesn't quite explain what happened. Otherwise we would expect to see the same phenomenon in other immigrant-heavy cities like São Paulo and New York during the early 1900s. Each of these cities indeed had a reduction in xenophobia—as measured by surveys of its citizens' fear of immigrants taking control or committing crimes—over time. But nowhere was as pronounced as Buenos Aires, nor as quickly.

Mere exposure effect happens a lot quicker with college students and mysterious black bags than it does with groups of people with long-standing fear of each other's religions. It wasn't enough to erase the deep-rooted anxieties in Buenos Aires in such a short amount of time. Mere exposure wouldn't be enough to make the folks at WebCT a team before nervous employees would decide to quit. And just being around unfamiliar women wasn't enough to explain how quickly Harbinger's Art of Charm alums overcame their fear of talking to them.

It turns out that Harbinger, the city of Buenos Aires, and soon Vallone, would tap into something even more powerful.

4.

In 2005, a motley group came together to work on a big project. There were over twenty of them, and each was an equal member of the work group—our third coalition of computer geeks.

They hailed from everywhere: Asia, Australia, Europe, and all corners of the United States from Tennessee to California. One member was a traveling salesman. Another was a university lecturer. One was a city bus driver. Another, a commercial airline pilot. There was a Chinese graduate student, an Indian researcher, a Caucasian real-estate agent. There was a grandfather, a young girl and her little brother, a bartender, a firefighter, a computer programmer, an architect, an engineer, a waiter, some high school students, a health spa worker, a veterinarian, and the stay-at-home wife of a soldier who was fighting in Iraq.

What task could bring such a team together? And where on earth would they convene?

It was actually not earth. They met in Azeroth, the fantasy realm dear to the hearts of all who play the online video game *World of Warcraft.**

The twenty-some-odd collaborators formed a "guild" of gamers— a ragtag team that took on missions in the game together. They knew each other only by their voices. They had only vague notions of their very different lifestyles and locations and levels of income. Some might have even avoided one another on the street, if they hadn't known better.

But they were here to play. And besides, Serpentshrine Cavern wasn't going to free itself from the reign of the evil Hydross the Unstable.

I don't want to get into too many details.† Simply put, MØndr@ke and Cylonluvr figured out that a warlock can basically kite the Lurker Below by throwing instant-speed dots and then just running up and down the stairs. But AngelNavio got jumpy and aggroed the coilfang frenzy way too soon, and the guild all thought they were cooked—until DocSnopes and Flutterbye cleared the last platform pack, and then it was the *coilfangs* who got cooked. So after that, they were basically just farming coilfang mobs. Morogrim Tide-walker was a grind, but he dropped the Luminescent Rod of the

---

*Full disclosure: I own, like, sixteen shares of stock in Activision Blizzard, which makes *World of Warcraft*. I bought those shares when I was in school and excited that *StarCraft II* was coming out. Please don't ask me how good I am at *StarCraft II*.

†I'm actually making up some of the details. But you get the idea. The broad strokes are accurate. And Hydross is indeed totally Unstable.

Naaru, and Hydross was cake after that. But then Jennikka9 said her mom was making her log out or she was grounded, so after that the raid was pretty much over.*

Over one hundred million players† around the globe have been citizens of Azeroth at one time or another. You might call it the world's fourteenth-largest country—beating Germany, the UK, and Egypt. Yet its players come from all those places and more. Contrary to the stereotype, *World of Warcraft* gamers are not basement-dwelling shut-ins with bad hygiene. They're doctors and bartenders and Delta pilots and—everyone.

Anthropologist Bonnie Nardi, a professor at the University of California, Irvine, took part in the raid on Serpentshrine Cavern. She was conducting an ethnographic study of the culture of online games and had joined a guild to get an inside peek at the phenomenon of collaboration that happens inside the game.

"One of the most striking things about *World of Warcraft* was the way it brought together social classes," Nardi observed in her book *My Life as a Night Elf Priest*. Nardi had spent her career conducting research on cultures around the world, and she'd come to expect general patterns of human behavior relating to in-groups fearing out-groups. In her travels, she'd personally confirmed psychologists' observations that humans' default mode was to collaborate with similar people and avoid or suspect different people. "When I was walking around villages in Papua New Guinea or Western Samoa," she said, for example, "I was obviously an outsider whose identity required explanation."

But *Warcraft* was different. In the game, there was neither fear

---

* Not a *Warcraft* gamer? How you are feeling right now is how I feel when people talk about college football.

† Blizzard announced in 2014 that 100 million player accounts had been created, with over 500 million characters created.

nor judgment for who she was. "In *Warcraft*," she said, "I was just another player."

World of Warcraft was a community where nobody needed to be afraid of who they were dealing with. It was a "magic circle," where players experienced, as Dutch historian Johan Huizinga put it, "a stepping out of 'real' life into a temporary sphere of activity," which takes the pressure of everyday anxieties away.

First published in 1938, Huizinga's oft-cited *Homo Ludens* broke ground in explaining what happens to our brains when we play— whether it's *Warcraft* or another game, or it's simply joking around. Play, according to Huizinga and later behavior scientists, is an absorbing experience where we escape from our regular social or physical obligations and experience pleasure. It becomes a refuge from real-world problems, danger, and fear.

And in recent years, neuroscientists have demonstrated that play and laughter can actually change our brains to be less fearful. How?

By tickling rats, of course.

In my entire life I never dreamed I'd hear the words "rat" and "tickle" in the same sentence. But there I was, on the phone with Jeffrey Burgdorf of Northwestern University. Burgdorf was the world's foremost expert on rat tickling.* He and his fellow researchers conducted experiments wherein they tickled rats to make them laugh.

My first question for Burgdorf was probably yours, too. "Why?"

---

*I can make this assertion because I believe he was at the time the world's *only* expert on rat tickling.

Because these weren't just any old rats, Burgdorf explained. "These rats are depressed."

Of course.

Depression, in the technical sense, is when one psychologically "gives up," Burgdorf explained. When you're depressed, you have a hard time engaging with the world—getting out of bed, working up the will to try. You can't see "the open door" to a potentially better future in front of you, and you shut down in a sort of fear-like apathy.

But getting rats to laugh, Burgdorf discovered, releases a chemical in the brain that "produces a rapid and robust antidepressant response." Laughing and playing can help to temporarily revitalize a rat who has stopped trying. In doing so, the rat becomes less paralyzed by the fear of the empty future its brain foresees. And after doing this a lot, it turns out, the neuroplasticity of the brain forms new pathways that helps the rat move forward.

Let me be clear: chronic depression is an insidious affliction. Millions of *humans* struggle with it every day, and laughter alone won't alleviate it for more than a moment. But Burgdorf's research is fascinating because it indicates how playing can physically help the brain to get braver. In other words, it hints at the brain science behind Huizinga's findings about how laughter and play can help our brains to "end a tension."

Do you see where we're going here?

When our brain perceives something scary, it goes on alert. The amygdalae fire up. This could be a dangerous object like that runaway minivan we talked about, or it could be the presence of a person who's different than us.

But when that violation turns out to be benign, the sudden realization has a cathartic effect. And so we breathe a sigh of relief, we laugh, and we go on.

Happening suddenly upon a bear, for instance, is scary. (I learned the hard way.) But finding out that it *isn't* a bear—it's just your friend Brian with his shirt off: that's a benign violation, and it makes you laugh. The amygdalae stand down; the hypothalamus holds off on the adrenaline. Everything's going to be okay.

This is exactly what playing does to us. As play theorist Dr. Brian Sutton-Smith says, "What we have in play is a simulation of an anxiety attack." Our amygdalae may start to get us riled up and alert, "but adrenaline is not being pumped into the system," Sutton-Smith says. "The frontal lobes win out over the reflexive phenomena in the back of the brain."

Play allows us, in other words, to become less afraid of things that might otherwise make us anxious. And that includes people from our out-group.

A New York University professor named Jay Van Bavel demonstrated this effect in a study wherein he showed photos of black people's faces and photos of white people's faces to a group of test subjects. Van Bavel scanned the test subjects' brains as they looked at the different faces. Predictably, the white test subjects' amygdalae were more active when they saw black people's faces—and vice versa. Neuroscience commonly finds this phenomenon with anyone who encounters someone of another race.

But then something interesting happened.

The test subjects were told they would be playing a game with the very people they were seeing in the photos.

When test subjects looked at the faces of fellow players, their amygdalae were more calm, regardless of what they looked like.

This happens in nature all the time, it turns out. Scientists have found that lemurs will play with lemurs from other kinship groups*

---

*A group of lemurs is called a conspiracy of lemurs. You read it. You can't unread it.

to get over xenophobia. Gorillas will play "tag" like human children to depressurize tense situations.

And that's what the millions of people who play *World of Warcraft* do.

A surprisingly large contingent of real-life military personnel play *World of Warcraft*, Nardi reports. And not because soldiers love war games.* They play, she said, to cope with the tension of actual war. "The game is escape," remarked a US Army soldier during one of Nardi's Azerothian campaigns. He said it helped to settle his fear.

Escape from outside tension isn't the only benefit of play. A 2008 study published in the *Harvard Business Review* confirmed what we've just discovered. It found that playing online games like *Warcraft* helps people become better collaborators across social divides. And not only that. The game also "gradually makes them less averse to group conflict."

Playing, it turns out, makes us less afraid of cognitive friction.

Harbinger and his coaches at Art of Charm thought they were helping their students overcome social fears through mere exposure. But the most powerful element of the program was play. The role-play in front of the camera with Suzanne was frightening, yes, but it was essentially a game. That made it easier to do. Gathering high fives at the bar? That was a game, too. The improv comedy was *nonstop* play.

Recast as play, threatening social interactions became social practice, like baby lions practicing how to hunt by play-wrestling

---

*And also not because of the well-established history of the US military using video games to recruit soldiers. In this particular case, at least.

with each other.* Playing helped depressurize situations that, for the students, were normally too scary to engage with. It helped them become comfortable with the inherent tension of social interactions that once drove them to shyness.

Just like it would help Carol Vallone's newlywed company stave off organizational silence.

5.

An old proverb says, "You can learn more about someone in an hour of play than in a year of talk."

Carol Vallone didn't have a year to spare. Her rival camps of programmers and educators were already digging trenches, preparing for segregation or war. She knew she had to do something.

So, at the new company's first conference in Vancouver, she strode onto the stage for her speech wearing pancake makeup, a feather boa, six-inch stilettos, and a two-tone bouffant.

She addressed her new company and its users as Cruella de Vil, the Disney villain, and facetiously announced that she was coming to ruin the old company. It was a hilarious acknowledgment of the worry on everyone's mind. "That," she said, "broke the ice."

Broke the ice. Broke the silence. With this little role-play, Vallone rendered a tense situation more benign. Her spoof made it

---

*I'm afraid this is also—not coincidentally—how some of Art of Charm's seedier counterparts teach men how to become so-called pickup artists. In my research for my magazine story, I learned that most of the dubious male specimens who style themselves pickup artists almost all start out afraid and unconfident when it comes to dating. The sordid pickup artist "community" helps these guys get over their reluctance by turning dating into a game. At the time of this writing, the arguably most well-known book on the topic of pickup artistry is in fact titled *The Game*.

easier for her employees to talk openly about what they'd been saying under their breath.

And Cruella de Vil was just the debut. Vallone set about creating a workplace permeated with play. She cross-relocated employees from one office to the other and restructured the company into rotating, cross-functional teams that not only had to work on projects together (and make use of the cognitive diversity that she "cast" on each team!), but also were to play together in a never-ending series of team games and competitions.

Teams competed to come up with funny internal code names for new products and features the company built. They made Olympic-style bids on what the theme of each company party would be. They prank-decorated the offices of employees who were out sick. They performed at all their conferences in costumed skits. They nominated each other for funny awards; when someone was caught doing an excellent job at something, her coworkers would tape a silly certificate to a barrel of pretzels and give a speech.

Some of the fun was more practical, but fun nonetheless. "There was a running competition that if your team could show that you could do something in a more cost-effective and collegial way, then you could have at it," Vallone said. One team figured out that instead of renting a block of hotel rooms for a company trip, they could rent a mansion for cheaper. So they did.

The new WebCT was a haven for jokes and costumes, fun rituals and made-up holidays. Contrast this with the scared silence of DaimlerChrysler's newly merged cultures. Playing created a "magic circle" where WebCT employees could fearlessly address the various elephants in their rooms. Play helped them feel like they were in the same in-group.

"It was part of the fabric of the organization," Vallone said. "It defuses angst. It defuses fear. It defuses worry."

When we step inside the magic circle of play, we leave real-world tension behind. And play, it turns out, doesn't just temporarily alleviate fear. Over time, it helps groups conquer it. As Pisa Group researchers Daniela Antonacci, Ivan Norscia, and Elisabetta Palagi point out, play "leads to the direct inhibition and regulation of aggression, thus improving social integration."

When we step out of the magic circle and return to real life, the players we've played with tend to stay in the "safe" category to our amygdalae. When we head to the locker room or log off the video game or wind up the improv session, we do so as members of the same "in-group."

Which is exactly what happened in Buenos Aires when the Jewish immigrants started playing soccer.

6.

During its first few decades in Argentina, *futbol* was a sport for the elite. Wealthy landowners played on manicured private football pitches.

But they weren't playing futbol in the barrio—not at first, anyway.

By 1920 the city's population was pushing two million. Half of all Porteños were born in other countries. Half of the rest were the children of immigrants.

The Western Europeans soon formed a distinct bloc—Italians, Germans, French, Spaniards, Britons, and even Scandinavians. These—sufficiently similar in appearance and religion—became an ambitious political minority. Argentina's ruling class worried about the country's national identity. What was an *argentino* anymore? As Buenos Aires grew, it was getting harder to answer that question with "gaucho."

Around this time, futbol made its way from the estate to the street. It was fast becoming the favorite sport of the working class. Kids started playing it on pavement. Futbol clubs popped up. Immigrants and nonimmigrants found themselves on the same street, or *cancha*, together. Their love for the Beautiful Game united them.

"Soccer introduced a national identity that was represented by the working class," writes David Goldblatt in *The Ball Is Round*, an epic nine-hundred-page history of the sport. "The Argentine football player and the Argentine football style became central icons of new notions of masculinity and the nation."

The celebrated gaucho gave way to the celebrated *"pibe"*:* the streetwise kid from the barrio; the one who gets by on sheer cunning and will. The pibe wasn't roping cattle from horseback. He was hooking a football. This was the new Argentine Dream: the rags-to-riches football god.†

Jewish gauchos were comparatively few, but what about Jewish pibes? Around the turn of the century, the roughly 120,000 Europeans of Jewish descent living in Buenos Aires were generally considered outsiders. They dressed and spoke and worshipped differently from other immigrant communities. They lived primarily in their own barrios, and they were seldom thought of as Argentinian.

But as futbol's popularity grew, Jewish children started playing it—among each other and with others from their out-group. And they didn't stop playing it as they grew up. By the 1920s futbol had become pastime *número uno* for Jewish Argentines. The cancha was common ground. Now there was something safe for everyone to make small talk about. Local newspapers were already portraying futbol as the new symbol of *porteñidad*—*porteño*-ness. Thus the Jewish footballer became *porteño*.

---

*Pronounced PEE-bay.

†The quintessential pibe is legendary *futbolista* Diego Maradona. As a child, Maradona once fell into a cesspool. He would later recall that the memory of his disgust was one of the things that drove him to succeed. Like Robert Diggs, Maradona found himself awash in literal shit. And, like Robert Diggs, Maradona had the courage to say ¡*Nunca más!*

Tel Aviv University professor Raanan Rein explains that belonging to a futbol club was a way for Jewish people to "become" Argentinian. Futbol, Dr. Rein writes,* was "a means of creating a new social identity."

Jewish Argentines didn't abandon their faith, of course. But in adopting Argentina's unofficial religion—and in joining with others to worship the almighty *gol*—Jewish Argentines made differences of faith and custom seem less scary. Public perception of Jewishness gradually became less hysterical.

Jewish Argentines were part of the in-group.

Barnard College historian José Moya writes that "Jewish residential segregation in Buenos Aires [. . .] dropped faster and sharper than in most other cities." Within a few years Jewish Argentines no longer needed to live shoulder to shoulder in order to feel safe. They soon dispersed into virtually every neighborhood in the city.

Were the Porteños really so exceptional? After all, Buenos Aires was hardly the only city in the Western Hemisphere to embrace futbol. The sport swept Latin America: São Paulo, Santiago, Mexico City— New World boomtowns with huge immigrant populations. While futbol helped depressurize tension between cultural groups in those cities as well, historians agree that the effect was more pronounced in Buenos Aires. Porteños simply became less fearful more quickly.

So why the difference?

Granted, the factors that drive social change are varied and complex. But in Buenos Aires, one factor is beyond dispute: participation in futbol was higher there than in any other city. Buenos Aires boasts the highest concentration of futbol clubs, and more people *play* per capita than anywhere in the world.†

---

*In *Fútbol, Jews, and the Making of Argentina*

†And they play through the good times and the bad. Argentina hosted and won its first World Cup in 1978 while political prisoners were being tortured by the country's tyrannical dictatorship.

"Societies where play (both with rules and without) is used in social practices," explain Antonacci, Norscia, and Palagi, "show a more fluid, democratic structure and are more open to new incomers." Play helps knock down social hierarchies by releasing the tension that prevents people from speaking up or out of turn. Even when play takes the form of win-or-lose competition, as long as the exercise is about the game and doesn't devolve into an exercise in destroying the other *people*, it has this camaraderie-building effect. And Buenos Aires had more of this effect than any comparable city in the world.

Play led to something of a virtuous cycle in Argentina. More futbol playing meant less segregation, which meant even more futbol playing and even less prejudice. As Professor Miles Hewstone of Oxford University found in a series of studies, city neighborhoods "with the most mixing between ethnic groups lead to the highest reductions in racial prejudice." And neighborhoods in the early-to-mid-twentieth century had less ethnic and racial segregation in Buenos Aires than any of its Brazilian, Chilean, or Mexican counterparts, because of soccer.

They were comfortable living together because they played together.

Of course play is no panacea for prejudice.* Xenophobia persists in Argentina as it does everywhere, futbol notwithstanding.† But in spite of this, modern Argentina still ranks high among nations in terms of tolerance and inclusivity.

---

*I am acutely aware of, and disgusted by, the racism, homophobia, and general hooliganism that stubbornly persist among some football/soccer fans, both in Latin America and worldwide. Fans have argued, for example, that homophobic cheers are merely a futbol tradition, with no meaning outside the game. This is a coward's explanation. I cordially defy anyone who claims that the magic circle of play sanitizes bigotry. Let's not let a few bad apples get away with abusing the magic of play this way. Love is love and hate is hate, on or off the field.

†Social labels are inherently problematic, but in today's clumsy parlance one might say that Argentina was always more "ethnically" diverse than "racially" diverse. Indeed, the country's low black population is due in part to President Bartolomé Mitre's racist policy of sending black men to die on the front lines during the Paraguayan War of 1865.

And Argentina's Jewish population? Over two hundred thousand, by most estimates. At the time of this writing there were about as many Jewish people in Argentina as in Haifa.*

In 2014, Pope Francis I staged a battle between representatives of the world's biggest religions. Jews and Christians; Hindus, Muslims, and Buddhists—the old pontiff pitted them one against another.

Why?

For charity. You see, Francis is Argentinian. He loved futbol and was hell-bent on watching devotees of the world's major religions go toe-to-toe on the field, with proceeds going to a good cause. The Pope had grown up knowing that play helps us get along.

"Tonight's match will . . . reflect on the universal values which football and sport in general can promote—loyalty, sharing, welcoming, dialogue, trust in the other," the Pope said. "It's about values which joins every person regardless of race, culture, and religious belief." †

It's not just sports that have this in-grouping effect on our brains. Play outside of sport can get the same psychological results. Antonacci and her colleagues teach that even unstructured play limits xenophobic aggression.

---

*And fun fact: in 1960, there were more Jewish people in Argentina than in Jerusalem.

† History's longest-standing peace accord came about in this way. When leaders of warring regions in the Peloponnese decided they wanted to stop fighting, they brought their people together peacefully through a series of games that are still being played today—the Olympics. The Olympics might have the longest track record, but sports were bringing communities together ages before the mere seventh century BCE. Indeed, many archaeologists believe the Lascaux cave paintings in France depict sprinting and wrestling matches from a community feast we missed by seventeen thousand years. Since at least the Stone Age, sports of all kinds have helped cities and communities and schools to bond.

And speaking of aggression, remember Wu-Tang? Those nine street-hardened lyrical warriors did not see themselves as an in-group at first. Robert Diggs knew their energy had the power to create—or to destroy—when first he hosted his in-house rap battle. And if we think about it, RZA's intramural competitions were actually a kind of game. That game helped enemies like Raekwon and Ghostface to bond. The circle worked its magic. Against the odds, Wu-Tang became a clan.

Now think about that fear-busting improv comedy—the secret sauce that helped the geeks at Art of Charm find their groove. By engaging in awkward play, shy guys started to see strangers for the first time as potential members of their own in-group, rather than as opponents or terrifying outsiders.

Dr. Nardi's *World of Warcraft* guild *thought* they were battling a luminous blue-green water monster. In fact, they were bridging social and geographical divides to an extent rarely seen in, say, a fractious UN General Assembly. No one had to sign a treaty. The guild's bridge building was simply the natural result of playing with different people.

When Argentines started playing futbol together, they became more comfortable with differences that had frightened them before. And as Argentina's national team got good—with players like Diego Maradona becoming world famous—play became something that enabled practically any two people in Argentina to have a conversation, no matter how different they appeared on the outside.

You'll recall how our friend Keith Yamashita likes to say that "micro-actions add up." Each of our stories of play reinforce this point. Vallone stabilized an unstable group through a thousand micro-opportunities. She set up an environment where her people could accumulate *lots* of little bonding moments in the Magic Circle together—and they became a great team through it. The sum of hundreds of positive, fun social interactions helped the Art of Charm geeks get better at being social, and they reported not just getting better at dating, but better at work, at networking, and at collaboration in general. And after thousands and thousands of encounters on the futbol cancha, the residents of Buenos Aires found a shared identity through play as well.

In all these cases, people who on paper should not have gotten along could now progress together in The Zone.

Overcoming fears and stabilizing group relationships is not the end, of course, to the challenge of making a great team tick.

In fact, sometimes our teams sit outside of The Zone, not because we have too much fear of conflict or too many problems with each other, but because things are going so well.

Or so we think.

QUATRO

―――⊕―――

ANGELIC TROUBLEMAKERS

"Take your best shot."

1.

On a September evening in 1887 in New York City, a five-foot-five brunette named Nellie mysteriously showed up at the front door of 84 Second Avenue, her pupils the size of saucers.

Her clothes were stylish, but old. A gray flannel frock. Brown silk gloves. A straw sailor's hat, and a gray veil. She had a low voice, a strange accent, and a distant look on her face. She carried no identification or personal effects.

The four-story brick building whose bell she rang was Matron Irene Stanard's Temporary Home for Females. For 30 cents, a working-class woman could stay the night in safety.

An attendant set Nellie up with a shared room and a meal, but by the end of dinner, something was clearly off.

The girl—nineteen years old and 112 pounds—seemed frightened, a "wild, hunted look in her eyes" according to the other women there that night. Nellie's story was strange. Upon questioning, she said she was from the American South and her last name was Brown. But she would later say she was from Cuba and her surname was Moreno. She had lost her trunks. She worried about all the murderers out there in the world, and all the people outside with so much work to do. She stared unblinking and whispered to herself over and over.

Around the time Nellie started asking if the other ladies in the home were insane, they decided she was dangerous. "I'm afraid to stay with such a crazy being in the house," said one.

Another declared, "She will murder us before morning."

Nellie didn't close her eyes all night. She stared at the bugs in the windowsill while the ladies phoned the police.

Two court appearances and three doctor's visits later, Nellie was lying on a bed at Bellevue Hospital, waiting to transfer to a mental asylum.

As she lay awake that night, Nellie heard the nurses talk about her and the other women. In the morning, a doctor asked her if she ever heard voices.

"Yes, there is so much talking, I cannot sleep," she replied truthfully.

"I thought so."

They declared Nellie "positively demented." She soon found herself walking a plank to the ferry that would take her to her new home.

"What is this place?" Nellie asked the man who escorted her off the boat.

"Blackwell's Island, an insane place, where you'll never get out of."

2.

Pablo Picasso was six years old when Nellie was committed to the insane asylum. It was only a few years later that his own mental health problems would begin.

He became severely depressed at twenty. His paintings for the next few years reflected this melancholy. They were washed out with blue.

Picasso managed his depression enough to become Spain's most famous painter—and soon the world's. But by the time he was sixty, his melancholy had worsened.

This led to a rather peculiar morning routine. As Picasso's lover at the time, Françoise Gilot (who was forty years his junior!), wrote in her memoir, "He always woke up submerged in pessimism." He'd lie in bed, groaning. Then, without fail, the following series of events would unfold:

His chambermaid would bring him his coffee and toast. Picasso would lie there, complaining. "Why get up? Why paint?" He was miserable. He was sick. Life was unbearable. He would stay under the covers for at least an hour, while Gilot pleaded with him to get up and paint.

"You're not so sick as that," she would say. "Your friends love you. Your painting is marvelous, everyone thinks so."

Picasso would eventually reply, "Well, maybe you're right . . . but are you sure?"

She would insist that she was. Finally, after a little more moaning, Picasso would drag himself out of bed and proceed to paint until dark.

And the next morning, the routine would start again.

Picasso painted more during the ten years he lived with Gilot than he did each decade before and after. During this period, he painted his famous Les Femmes d'Alger series, the last painting of which set a world record at auction in 2015, selling for $179 million.

We'd be justified in theorizing that this wouldn't have happened if Gilot had not coaxed Picasso out of bed.

This little story teaches us something more than how to get a depressed painter to pick up his brush. Often we have all of the ingredients we need to do amazing work, but we are metaphorically stuck in bed.

This is what happens when we don't have any cognitive friction on our teams. We may have all sorts of differences available for the harnessing, but we're not making use of them.

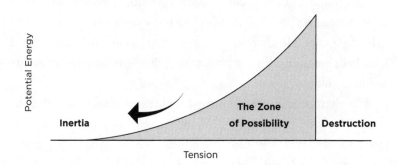

When it comes to team dynamics, depression isn't usually the culprit that puts us in the Inertia Zone. More often than not, the problem is—ironically—prior success.

The more successful we are using a set of perspectives and heuristics, the more inflexible our brains become on that particular topic. Psychologists call this "cognitive entrenchment."

People get cognitive entrenchment the longer they work on the same things in the same ways—and especially when those ways work. Research shows us that the longer people work together, the more similar their work styles tend to become. We may start out different, but the more time we spend together, the more we start speaking, behaving, and even dressing similarly. After a while, our perspectives have a tendency to converge. We learn and mimic each other's heuristics. Over time, it is easy for us to get stuck in the same patterns of thinking. The business world often calls them "best practices," but psychologists correctly call them "groupthink." And groupthink, as we've learned, eliminates cognitive friction. We find good solutions on Problem Mountain and then settle down on them.

Research by Erik Dane, professor at Rice University, sums up the resulting irony: "Because of cognitive entrenchment, experts may be restricted in their ability to identify optimal solutions to problems, to adapt to novel situations, and to generate radically creative ideas within their domain."

In other words, often the things that keep us stuck on a mountain peak are our own expert perspectives and heuristics that got us there in the first place.

In these cases, like our Picasso story hints at, the thing that holds us back from our Dream Team potential is the lack of a teammate who can give us a certain kind of nudge.

3.

On the first night inside Blackwell's Island, Nellie shivered uncontrollably.

The facilities were freezing. Inmates stood in hallways chattering from the New York cold. When Nellie asked for a nightgown, the nurse replied, "You don't need to expect any kindness here, for you won't get it." She was doused in freezing water, scrubbed roughly, and forced to clean the nurses' quarters.

The asylum had opened up in 1839, next door to the prison built there a few years earlier. It was the first city-run mental asylum, part of a push to provide living space and round-the-clock care for the mentally ill—and to keep them separate from the public.

By the time Nellie got to Blackwell's, the number of committed patients around the country had shot up to 150,000. New York had several packed asylums at this point.

Lunacy had become an excuse to lock away anybody that society didn't want around. Vagrants and paupers were routinely thrown into the asylum without having committed a crime. Worse, any woman deemed "unruly" or who voiced strong opinions could be sent to the asylum on the word of a husband or brother. They were locked up with the schizophrenics.

Asylums like Blackwell's were notoriously underfunded and understaffed. But officials like New York City mayor Abram Hewitt gave little priority to the matter—or even much thought. Hewitt was busy working on tax reform and planning the development of the subway system.

So for fifty years, the mental asylum system had run itself. And that was how New Yorkers liked it. Places like Blackwell's Island kept unwanted neighbors, as the saying goes, out of sight and out of mind.

But in its decades-long inertia, the asylum system and its patients were going nowhere. Society had found a mountain peak and set up camp on it for good. Low standards were not improving. Patients like Nellie found themselves in prison-like conditions that offered little chance of help or pain relief—where the world no longer had to think about them.

Nellie had appeared disoriented and confused that night at Matron Stanard's. But she had not done anything particularly dangerous. Regardless, her strangeness and paranoia sent threat signals to
the collective amygdalae of the ladies at the shelter. Her unusual way
of speaking and thinking bothered the police who subsequently
dealt with her. So they locked her away.

Something was indeed off about Nellie. But it wasn't what the
Blackwell's staff thought.

4.

The G-Corp executives were flabbergasted.*
They congregated in a spacious, exposed brick loft in central
London, eyes wide. The setting was the office of Sense Worldwide,
a consulting firm tasked with helping expand the market for one of
G-Corp's struggling products.

The product was the "blister cushion"—a bandage that released
ointment into a wound over time. Several years after blister cushion's invention in the 1980s, sales had plateaued. G-Corp, a giant
health goods company with products found in every major pharmacy
in the world, couldn't figure out how to make its blister cushion line
grow. The company sat in the Inertia Zone, like Picasso lounging in
his bed.

It wasn't like G-Corp hadn't tried to get out of bed, though. It
had explored a few ideas here and there. But the company couldn't
come up with anything better than the existing blister cushion product. Or at least nothing that attracted more customers.

---

*For confidentiality purposes, I've changed the actual name of the company.

Dr. Dane's research on cognitive entrenchment describes this scenario exactly. When we have a solution that has worked well for a long time, it becomes difficult to see any other way. "Problem solvers can become fixated on a particular method to their own detriment," he says.

That's why G-Corp had hired the Sense team, led by a man named Brian Millar, a British writer and game designer. He specialized in helping companies find radically better mountain peaks, so to speak.

After assessing the situation, Millar told the G-Corp execs to come by his office to talk with a focus group about blisters. Little did they know, Millar had a surprise prepared.

Instead of random demographically diverse people recruited from the mall—the kind of typical focus group that people at G-Corp would be used to—a group of beautiful women filed into Sense's office. They sported long hair, makeup, and painted fingernails. And instead of shopping bags, they brought with them an array of spiky leather boots and heels.

They were professional dominatrices.

As the ladies took their seats, the executives shook their heads. This was not G-Corp's target customer. People who got paid to sexily whip other people were not who they had in mind when they'd told Millar they wanted to expand their customer base. All the dominatrices in the world could only buy a tiny fraction of the blister cushions G-Corp wanted to sell. What kind of gimmick was this?

The history of focus groups dates back to World War II, when psychologists had people watch military propaganda films. The doctors would hide behind one-way glass to observe which messages were most persuasive to the average person. They wanted to know what kinds of language and imagery might best influence people.

After the war, a different kind of propagandist took up this practice: marketers.

Companies began recruiting people to test which products and campaigns were the most persuasive to the largest number of potential customers. These "focus groups" soon evolved into a way for companies to get inspiration for what to do in the first place. If you're out of ideas, why not ask everyday people what they want, and then make it?

Brian Millar's agency existed in part because these kinds of focus groups have a big problem: everyday people tend to come up with everyday ideas.

"Most average consumers are actually pretty happy with the product they've got," Millar explained to me. "I was very happy with my late-nineties Nokia," he says. "If you'd said, 'What new features could we add to your phone?' I would have said, 'This phone is perfect. I can't help you with that.'"

Our amygdalae will often cause us to be uncomfortable with exactly the kinds of ideas that focus groups are supposed to come up with. Anything creative or different is going to feel foreign, even scary. Studies find this in business all the time. In fact, people who introduce creative ideas, according to research led by Jennifer Mueller of the University of Pennsylvania, are less likely to be listened to or made leaders. That's because "the expression of creative ideas is often associated with uncertainty."

This explains the list of things that bombed in focus group research, according to Millar: PCs, Pop-Tarts, *Seinfeld*, nachos, and Aeron chairs. People didn't like them. Until they got used to them, messy cheese chips and neurotic New York sitcoms were uncomfortable concepts for many people.

The Aeron chair is an excellent example, actually. For ages, business executives sat in big leather chairs. Aeron chairs, by contrast, were thin, low profile, and made out of mesh. So even though Aerons were more comfortable, flexible, and breathable, focus groups rejected them. A silly-looking chair with tiny holes in it was a threat to an executive's powerful appearance. It made her look like part of the out-group.

Aeron's popularity, therefore, started with people on the fringes. "The people who really liked them were very petite women, very obese people, and elderly people," Millar explains. "Because you could get in and out of them very fast, because your skin breathes, and because they were so super adjustable." Little by little, average business-people became exposed to Aeron through these not-so-average chair users. And little by little the chair became less threatening.

So, despite completely failing in focus groups, Aeron went on to become the best-selling office chair in the world.

Instead of focus groups of average people, Aeron needed people with a more extreme perspective. It turned out that a very large or very small person could tell you more about the problems with office chairs than a very powerful person could.

"People who have those extreme needs are often the people who are the most articulate about things," Millar said. They're like someone who's staring up from the foot of a giant mountain on the Problem Mountain range. Their extreme perspectives help them see farther through the fog.

This is why, Miller explained, if you're trying to make a better insect repellent, you won't get as much from a focus group full of vacationers as you will by talking to people who live in shantytowns.

"Somebody once said to me, 'Some days I have to choose between buying insect repellent and buying food. For a day my kids can live off a little bit of rice, but I can't go a day without insect repellent, because if my kids get dengue, they might die,'" Millar recalled. "That's somebody who will happily sit for three hours and tell you all of their issues with the current repellents on the market. They can tell you how to make a better one." That's somebody you want on your team.

After introducing the G-Corp executives to the dominatrices, Millar distributed Sharpie markers. He then made the executives kneel in front of the focus group members and draw circles around their blister spots.

This was not comfortable. But that was part of Millar's point. G-Corp had been in the Inertia Zone for so long that its team needed a push.

They needed to experience an extreme perspective on blisters, Millar said. And who has more to say about the way a blister bandage looks and feels than someone who has to wear complicated, tortuous heels to work, and whose feet are inspected closely by their clients?

The executives got the point. But that was not the end of the focus group. To their surprise, a crew of Special Forces soldiers tromped its way through the doors. That's because, Millar said, if you asked the question, "Who thinks ten times as much about blisters than a health care executive?" the answer would not be, "Random shoppers from the mall." It would be something like, "A person who has to run ten miles a day through the desert in combat boots."

Millar's tactic—bringing in extreme people to focus groups instead of average ones—is a clever way to get cognitive diversity. If we return to Problem Mountain, a dominatrix or Special Forces soldier is someone who looks at the problem of blisters like this:

These people had spent more time than anyone exploring the blister mountain range, and thus developed a unique perspective on it. They could see the biggest mountains that the blister makers couldn't. And to deal with those big mountains, they'd developed heuristics that could give G-Corp's product designers a path forward.

The soldiers articulated an entire spectrum of type and severity of blister that one can have, depending on how the blister formed and how many days old it was. The dominatrices explained how they would cut and alter blister bandages into shapes that worked with their shoes and fit around the curves of their feet and ankles and still looked good.

G-Corp developed a new line of blister pads of different shapes and thicknesses based on what the dominatrices showed them. They made pads for different blister ages and severities based on what the soldiers taught them.

And it turned out that when you offered these types of blister pads to "average" people, they bought more of them. By tapping into the cognitive diversity of "extreme consumers," G-Corp managed to find better solutions for regular consumers.

And they started making more sales again.

There's an important thing we should note about this story. Millar could have interviewed dominatrices and soldiers and summarized their ideas in a report for G-Corp. But he didn't. He made the executives get on their hands and knees and draw circles around people's blisters with Sharpies. A key part of his extreme focus group exercise is the theater of having his clients experience them firsthand.

That's because sometimes being aware of the path up the mountain is not enough. Sometimes we need to be pushed into The Zone, provoked to get off our peak, so we have no choice but to either retreat or make progress. G-Corp was paying Millar, in part, because he was the team member they needed to nudge them out of their comfy chairs.

5.

Blackwell's Island Insane Asylum wasn't just cold, Nellie quickly discovered. It was disgusting.

The food was unpalatable: hard black bread with insects, inedible butter, and rotting prunes. The tea tasted like copper.

The nurses were crude and rough. Attendants mocked, slapped, and choked the inmates. They "expectorated tobacco juice" and berated the patients when they weren't gossiping about the doctors in front of them.

Nellie was locked in a room at night with six women, one who raved and paced all night and several others who seemed perfectly sane.

Nellie tried to tell the doctors that she wasn't crazy. But the more she tried, the more convinced they were that she was nuts.

"What are you doctors here for?" she inquired.

"To take care of the patients and test their sanity," an exasperated caretaker replied.

"Very well," Nellie said. "There are sixteen doctors on this island, and excepting two, I have never seen them pay any attention to the patients. How can a doctor judge a woman's sanity by merely bidding her good morning and refusing to hear her pleas for release? Even the sick ones know it is useless to say anything, for the answer will be that it is their imagination."

They told her to shut up.

6.

D r. Charlan Nemeth of UC Berkeley spent her career studying the science of human influence. Specifically, she's an expert on how people with minority viewpoints can influence others.

Typically, when a team comes together to make a decision, the majority opinion wins out. But in the 1970s, Nemeth became interested in what kinds of influence people who disagreed with the majority had on group decision making—such as juries deciding whether someone was guilty of a crime or not.

She put together a bunch of experiments to find out. In one, she assembled groups of six people at a time to work on little puzzle-like challenges together. The object was to determine if there was a "hidden figure" inside whatever they were looking at.

What she found was surprising. Groups of people who tended to agree that there was no hidden figure on a given challenge were sometimes correct, and sometimes not. But groups that had one or two people who often disagreed with the majority opinion ended up getting more answers right. Having a naysayer in the group made the rest of the group think harder.

This should remind us of what we saw with our cops of different genders. Having someone with a different perspective helps the rest of the group think more critically. The subtlety that Dr. Nemeth discovered is that the person who thinks differently doesn't always have to have the right answer for the group to get smarter. She or he just has to be a little difficult.

Nemeth's experiments went on to show that the presence of a minority viewpoint—at least one person who vocally disagrees with the common perspective—tends to help groups look at issues "on all sides." Meanwhile, groups that are very similar and have no dissenters tend to look for information "that corroborated the majority view." In other words, when we are on the same page, we tend to see things that prove that we're right. When we're not on the same page, we become more likely to see parts of the picture we've missed.

"Dissenting views by a minority of individuals," Nemeth writes, "stimulate the kinds of thought processes that, on balance, lead to better decisions, better problem solving, and more originality."

Notice the word choice here. Dissenters *stimulate* the kinds of thought processes that lead to progress. They shake us. Spur us. They do for inert groups what play does for chaotic groups—move us into The Zone.

We might call this process "provocation":

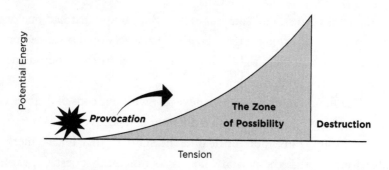

Provocateurs are people who force us out of inertia—like Gilot did to get Picasso out of bed, or Millar did to get the G-Corp execs off their comfortable mountain peak with their blister cushions. Whether it comes from our in-group or out-group, provocation stretches the rubber band.

In 2009, a group of researchers recruited a bunch of sorority and fraternity members from colleges for a study. Frats and sororities are notoriously good at cultivating conformity in their groups. It's kind of the point. So their members are perfect candidates for experiments involving in-group and out-group interactions, and in this case, what can help a tight-knit in-group break out of its group-think.

First, the students were given twenty minutes to study a murder mystery. Then they were placed in groups of three people from their own frat or sorority to decide together who the murderer was. After twenty minutes, each group was joined by a fourth person— either from within their same frat or sorority, or from a different one.

What the researchers found was that having an outsider join the group led to team members feeling less comfortable, more agitated, and less confident in their answers. And it also led them to *double* their chance of getting the right answer.

The work felt harder when the groups were joined by an outsider.

And that was precisely what helped those groups find better solutions.

Provocateurs, in other words, push us off our mountain peak. Sometimes this just makes life difficult. But sometimes it helps us discover that there's a taller peak just ahead.

7.

Before they sent her to the asylum, the doctors at Bellevue had labeled Nellie "the most peculiar case that ever came into the hospital."

That may be because she was only pretending to be insane.

"Nellie" was actually a twenty-three-year-old woman named Elizabeth Jane Cochran. To the public, she was Nellie Bly, a reporter for the *New York World*, run by Joseph Pulitzer.

For years, Blackwell's had a reputation for poor conditions, but nobody besides the nurses and inmates had been able to get a close look. Not even city officials knew what was really happening there. And no one was working hard to find a better way to take care of its patients.

After ten days at Blackwell's Island, Bly had gathered enough firsthand material for a tell-all report. Pulitzer rescued her from the asylum and published her seventeen-chapter exposé, which took over editions of the *New York World*.

"The insane asylum on Blackwell's Island is a human rat-trap," Bly summarized. "It is easy to get in, but once there it is impossible to get out."

Some 1,600 women occupied Blackwell's Island Asylum, and many of them were not crazy, she revealed. For example, one woman had been suffering from an illness that made her hair fall out. She was committed for not much more than her unusual appearance. Another woman, who spoke only German, was there because a doctor simply hadn't been able to communicate with her. Another woman had been locked up after having gotten sick at a breakfast. And hundreds had been locked up just for disagreeing with the men in their lives.

The nurses were unqualified. (One reported the temperature of an inmate to be 150 degrees!) The doctors flirted inappropriately. And until Nellie Bly, hardly anybody gave Blackwell's or the mental health system a thought.

The system was a "success" in the public's eyes.

That's why Bly's series shook New York City Hall so hard. The severe condition of the asylum underscored the need for funding and reform at every stage of the mental health care system. Bly's story was an act of investigative journalism—a practice she helped pioneer—that proved to be the provocation the city needed to take a fresh look at things. It resulted in a grand jury hearing, after which New York City apportioned $1 million to fixing Blackwell's Asylum. Not long after, the whole asylum system was replaced with a more humane and effective national mental hospital program.

The doctors at Blackwell's were ashamed and furious when Bly's report came out. But it was too late. The public—and the government— had been pushed out of bed. Whether they wanted to or not, they now saw mental health care from a new perspective. The only reasonable thing to do now was to search for a better mountain peak.

If it had been up to Blackwell's, Bly would have been punished for sneaking into the asylum and exposing them. They would blame her instead of seeing what they needed to see from her. Fortunately, the government had established a process for allowing provocateurs like Bly to help with civic progress in this way: through the US Constitution's right to a free press.

In America, the press is often referred to as the fourth branch of government. When the founders set up the executive, judicial, and legislative branches as the team that makes up the government, they created explicit protection for the press in the First Amendment of the Bill of Rights—because they knew that the press would be an essential teammate for a functioning democracy.

Investigative journalism's goal, as the saying now goes, is provocation in a nutshell: to "comfort the afflicted, and afflict the comfortable." It shows us perspectives that we don't see so we can break out of inertia. Provocation like this can indeed be uncomfortable, but it's an important piece of how the American republic has fought off corruption and made progress in many areas where other free nations have not.*

The American founders had the foresight to set their team up this way. I'd dare say this is how we ought to think about setting up any good team. Continual progress depends on leaders making it safe for provocateurs to make waves, for whistle-blowers to raise their hands, and for dissenters to speak up when needed.

Provocation prods an inert group into The Zone. It helps us to stretch the rubber band. This means that, contrary to our instinct, the collaborator who provokes or contradicts us is our ally. As Dr. Nemeth puts it, "One must learn not only to respect and tolerate dissent, but to 'welcome' it."

---

*The Pulitzer Prizes reward, among other things, investigative journalism that provokes change. Since Bly, journalists have exposed corruption from Watergate to water poisoning, from gun smuggling to illegal eavesdropping. And Bly herself went on to become one of the most influential journalists and women's rights activists in history.

There are a few ways to do this. We can "cast" team members who will push us to think or work harder than we would otherwise, like Gilot did to Picasso, or Coach Tikhonov did to the Russian Five.* We can also invite outsiders with extreme perspectives to show us things we won't be able to unsee afterward—like Brian Millar did with the G-Corp folks.† And we can bring dissenters into our fold with the explicit instruction to tell us what's up, like the US founders set up with the free press.‡

Once we start thinking of provocation as helpful, it changes the way we deal with it.§ In 2016, the Pentagon made a good example of itself in this regard. Though the Pentagon boasts to have the best computer security in the world, it did something many organizations would never dream of. It invited a group of hackers to try to poke holes in its systems.

The hackers, recruited by the company HackerOne, found the first security hole in thirteen minutes. They found 138 vulnerabilities in all.

"It proved to the skeptics who believed hackers are dangerous, childish, and intentional lawbreakers," said Department of Defense agent Lisa Wiswell, that instead, hackers can be "extremely helpful." By inviting provocateurs in, the Pentagon was able to build a better

---

*In my life as a journalist, this role is often played by an editor who says, "Make it even better," or "Make it shorter." In my role as a company owner, it was often my partner Dave, who could be relied on to say, "I don't think so" or "Why?" no matter what I was proposing.

†As a writer, I'll often run my work-in-progress by a friend who hates books, and also my know-it-all buddy who has Goodreads and the IMDB memorized. In business, it was helpful to interview both people who are adamant about never buying a product like ours as well as people whose problems were so big they thought no one could solve them.

‡In my own work I like to periodically ask my biggest critics to tear me apart, or to hypothesize how they would destroy my work. This requires being willing to feel pain, but it's useful.

§An important key to dealing with provocation is to parse sweeping critiques aimed at our identity (e.g., "I am bad"), which aren't helpful and usually inaccurate, from actionable critiques (e.g., "My power generator has one-tenth the range").

computer system. The project led the US Army to hire HackerOne hackers to do the same. "Take your best shot," Secretary of the Army Eric Fanning told them when the project started.

Legendary civil rights leader Bayard Rustin, the man behind the 1963 March on Washington, once declared, "We need, in every community, a group of angelic troublemakers." He was right. We need the dissenters, the whistle-blowers, the critics, and the extreme perspectives to help us get us out of inertia and into The Zone—and we need leaders who make it safe for them to do it.

This is how we make progress when we're stuck.

But how far does this idea go? What about people who *are* mentally ill? Can teams benefit from including people who aren't just pretending to be insane? Or people whose ideas are *actually* crazy?

It turned out that I was about to see for myself.

ПЯТЬ

———◉◉———

THE BLACK SQUARE

"His best friend is his clever but lazy dog
that has the bad habit of urinating on Patrik's rug."

1.

Mark Tigan, civil servant of the village of Winooski, Vermont, was thirty-two years old when the president of the United States called to shut him down.

This was 1979. Tigan was a bit of a wunderkind in the field of small-town city planning. Having graduated as one of the nation's first environmental studies majors at San Jose State, he'd developed a reputation for his enthusiasm for community projects. He'd even been on national television, in a Walter Cronkite report showing him burying automobiles to protest carbon emissions. Now he'd been put in charge of Winooski's staff of city planners to try to boost its struggling economy.

With a population of seven thousand, Winooski was a blip on the map. The town was nestled in the shadow of its across-the-river neighbor, Burlington, which, though beautiful and known for its recently launched ice cream brand, Ben & Jerry's, wasn't very big, either. Burlington was the smallest city in any US state that was also that state's biggest city.

Anyway. Nobody knew that Winooski existed until after the night Tigan and his staff got drunk.

Winooski was cold. Temperatures regularly reached twenty below. Its downtown area had just a couple of bars and a restaurant called Winooski Restaurant. These sat next to a handful of abandoned mills and factories from New England's proud, lost industrial days.

The world outside was facing an industrial crisis of its own. Iran was in the middle of a revolution, with its shah having fled and massive protests and strikes slashing its oil refinery production. Global oil prices had doubled in less than a year. American gas stations had long lines. And the cost to heat Winooski had risen to $4 million a year—$14.2 million in 2018 dollars. By one calculation, heat for a family of three would cost more than $500 a month in 2018 money.

Burlington had just put in a request for government funds to build a hydroelectric plant along the river to help reduce its own heating bill. This plan, however, would leave Winooski's creek bed dry. "Basically, ruin our downtown," Tigan told me. With already high unemployment and declining commerce, Winooski might be done for.

It was amid this turmoil that Tigan took his staff out for a drink and a chat. How could the city-planning office pitch in to help their struggling town? One bottle of wine turned into two. Someone complained about the temperature. Someone else mentioned wishing they could "put a lid" on Winooski to keep the heat in. And that's when Tigan came up with the bad idea of a lifetime.

"What if we built a dome over the city?"

Everyone was tipsy by then. They all thought it was a good plan.

A week later, Tigan left for Washington, DC, on business. On the way, he stayed the night in Baltimore. There he told his dome idea to a buddy who worked as a liaison between Congress and the Department of Housing and Urban Development. "You know . . . ," his friend said. "The assistant secretary, Bob Embry, loves domes." Dome houses had become briefly popular during the '60s and '70s for their energy efficiency and structural integrity. Though they were funny looking, it was easier to heat a dome than a rectangular home and hard for an earthquake to knock one down. By this time, however, dome fever had faded alongside tie-dye and Pet Rocks, except among a few diehards. Embry was apparently one of them.

As fate would have it, Tigan's friend was supposed to carpool with Embry and two other HUD people to Washington the next day. "I'll call and cancel," he said. "You take my spot."

During the carpool, Tigan pitched Assistant Secretary Embry his idea to save oil costs by putting Winooski under a big, clear dome. They could make it with air locks for cars to enter—like a space station—and lower heating expenses like crazy. The frigid town could grow tomatoes all year-round.

Embry was the exact right person to say this to. He turned around from the front seat. "If you propose that, I'll fund it," he declared, according to Tigan. "I have discretionary funding."

Tigan delivered the news to his flabbergasted staff. They eagerly put together a report and proposal.

Winooski's mayor asked, "Are you nuts?" But when Tigan explained that this could mean millions in HUD funding, the city council signed on.

The dome story blew up. The day after the Burlington newspaper wrote about that council meeting, three television trucks showed up to Winooski City Hall. National newspapers followed. *Time* magazine called for an interview.

The Vermonters had few answers for the inevitable questions. They made up specifics on the fly. How high would it be? "Uh . . . two hundred fifty feet!" What about automobile exhaust? "We'll have electric cars or monorails inside!"

Bags of mail started arriving from dome weirdos. An International Dome Symposium was scheduled in Winooski, where the famous crackpot inventor R. Buckminster Fuller would give a keynote.

Nobody had built a dome this big before. Nobody knew what it would be made out of. Would it have giant support struts? Would the town be pressurized like a balloon to hold it up? What if the dome deflated and fell on everyone? How was the city going to justify annexing the land surrounding the town that would be needed for the dome walls?

It soon became clear that building and maintaining a dome large enough to fit Winooski, engineered to keep the heat in *and* not kill everyone, would probably cost a lot more than the heating bill savings it would generate. Plus it would, you know, ruin the view.

National newspapers wrote about what a bad idea the dome was. David Letterman mocked it on his show. There was even a song made about it, "Dome over Winooski," making fun of the plan:

> *Dome over Winooski*
> *Not far from the lake*
> *Transparent and lasting*
> *Still real and not fake.*
> *Dome over Winooski*
> *So fair and so true*
> *Has anyone asked you*
> *What's cooking with you?*

"The research money might give one guy a job," said Hank Tetreault, co-owner of Winooski Restaurant, to the *Christian Science Monitor.* "Maybe he will eat here."

The Winooski Dome soon became one of the top news stories in Saudi Arabia. Some in the Middle East started to panic about how America was putting cities under domes in order to stick it to the oil industry.

That's around the time HUD assistant secretary Embry's phone rang.

"What the hell are you doing?"

It was President Carter. He was running a tough election campaign against Ronald Reagan. International ridicule about the federal government paying millions to cover towns in Vermont with domes was not helping. The conversation, according to Tigan, ended with a presidential order: "You've got to pull this."

2.

We've been talking about the power of cognitive diversity for half a book now. In the last chapter we discussed how provocation, dissenting viewpoints, and "angelic troublemakers" are often what we need to get a team thinking critically again. But the Winooski Dome story reminds us of an important reality: some "different" ideas, frankly, are quite bad.

"The more perspectives we collectively possess, the better our chances" of making a breakthrough together, points out our friend Dr. Page from earlier. But, he adds, "just because someone brings a different perspective doesn't mean that it will lead to a better solution."

Any perspective—even one that might seem crazy—has the potential to be useful under the right circumstances. But that doesn't mean that it *will* be. So the question we're going to explore in this chapter is: How can a team or its leaders discern when it should seriously consider a different way of thinking, and when it's a waste of time?

After all, a city covered by a geodesic dome was a good idea somewhere. That place just happened to be Mars.*

The perspective of a young activist who'd had a few drinks was

---

*And the jury's still out on whether that's a good idea.

unfortunately not one that could help cold old Winooski with its heat trouble and battle over its river. Thirty-two-year-old eco-warrior Mark Tigan's cognitive diversity was just a little too far-out to be of any use.

Or was it?

3.

After tromping through Moscow's streets for a bit more than an hour, I'd finally gotten out of the dreary March drizzle and into the massive Tretyakov Gallery, one of the biggest art museums in the world.

I was standing in one of its vaulted rooms, looking at another dumb idea.

This one was possibly even more expensive than Mark Tigan's dome. Though it was much smaller.

As a member of the creative industry, I believed in the power of art to convey meaning and ideas. And I could appreciate that some things we create are simply about beauty for beauty's sake. But even I had to admit that some art was hard to find something good to say about.

Case in point: the 79.5-centimeter-square painting that I had just traversed Moscow to see.

My problem with this particular painting was that it somehow managed to be one of art critics' favorites, while at the same time regular people seemed to think it was ridiculous. Even my friends with fine arts degrees in New York could find little to say about it other than it was "famous" and "old."

On the other hand, scholars like Phillip Shaw of the Tate Modern said things like this:

"The experience of viewing the painting involves a feeling of pain brought about by the breakdown of representation followed by a powerful sense of relief, even elation, at the thought that the formless or massive can nevertheless be grasped as a mode of reason."

New Yorker writer Peter Schjeldahl called the painter's touch, "ineffable sweetness." He said, without irony, that the art was made with "a shudder of the sublime."

Meanwhile, people on the Internet said things like, "I could have done that in kindergarten."

The hype around this painting confused me so thoroughly that I'd gone through the hoops of getting a Russian visa to check it out. In the interest of open-mindedness, I'd decided that perhaps seeing the painting in person would help me understand.

And so, I braved winter, customs, and possible future invitations to join President Donald Trump's cabinet (this joke will surely expire at some point!), to investigate.

The Tretyakov Gallery has several buildings and thousands of paintings. There are meticulous landscapes and still lifes so realistic that I sometimes mistook them for photographs. Oil paintings of every boat, animal, and historical figure ever produced by Russia. A family of bears playing in the woods. Knights on horses. Dead knights after battles. And a hundred gorgeous, gold-foil, Renaissance-era Jesuses. There's even a portrait of a Russian John Goodman with a white corsage, hanging next to a Russian Zach Galifianakis in a vest lounging on a red-and-white-striped beanbag.

Somewhere in Building 4, I turned a corner, and there it was in the center of a cavernous room.

I sat in front of it for an hour.

While soaking it in, I noticed something. Most of the museum-goers who came in ignored the painting. An elderly couple holding hands hesitated in front of it, then walked on. Two young lovers took photos of each other in front of every other painting in the room, but decided not to with this one. A portly gentleman beelined past it toward a couple of paintings of young women.

Clearly, the visitors that day experienced neither shudder nor sweetness from Russia's most infamous painting.

Perhaps that's because the painting is just a big, black square.

That's it.

Seriously. A black square. Nothing else. Just, you know, black paint. Painted in a square.

It's not even that big, to be honest. It's like one of those old televisions where the screen is fifteen inches and the wooden box around it is twenty-six.

I took a video on my phone as a dark-haired teenager in a turquoise top looked at the painting's title plaque, which said—wait for it—*Black Square*. She made a face that said, "What?," and moved on to some more exciting paintings, which was all of them.

Her reaction was a much simpler way of putting another part of Mr. Shaw's outrageous review: "The failure of the black square to represent this transcendent realm serves 'negatively' to exhibit the 'higher' faculty of reason, a faculty that exists independent of nature."

In other words, the point of the *Black Square* is, literally, nothing.

On the way to Moscow, I'd picked up a book about the *Black Square* at London's Royal Academy of Arts—with the appropriately snobby subtitle, *The Climax of Disclosure*—in the hopes of finding some sort of explanation for this painting of nothing. That's when I decided that its creator, Kazimir Malevich, was out of his mind.

He was born in Ukraine in 1878 to poor parents and made his way to Moscow to seek his fortune as an artist. After dabbling in Impressionism he started painting faceless people and getting bizarrely spiritual about it.

"What we call Reality is infinity without weight, measure, time or space, absolute or relative, never traced to become a form," he wrote, around 1920. "It can be neither represented nor comprehended."

The stuff he said got more bizarre—and detailed—over the years. Here's another example:

"Stimulus is a cosmic flame that lives in what is non-objective: only in the skull of thought does it become cool in real concepts of its immeasurableness; and thought, as a certain degree in the action of stimulus, white-hot in its flame, moves deeper and deeper into the infinite, creating its path worlds of the universe."

Reality isn't real. Cosmic flames stimulate the universe. Got it.

Malevich eventually tried to start a spiritual art movement called suprematism. The idea was to find "the zero point of painting." The very edge of the artistic spectrum, beyond which nothing else existed.

The *Black Square* was his master work. It was, he claimed, the point where art ended. Anyone who continued beyond would fall off a cliff, like those old maps when the world was still flat.* There was no art that said "nothing" better than the *Black Square*.

New Yorker writer Tatyana Tolstaya called this "one of the most frightening events in art in all of its history of existence."

It wasn't frightening, though. It was quadrilateral.

If the purpose of art was to be as beautiful as possible, I had just found a very low point on the mountain range. If the purpose of art was to communicate ideas, the *Black Square* is one of the most exotic perspectives I can think of. It was off the range. To an average person with an average perspective on art, the mountain diagram of Malevich's work might look like this:

---

*Here be dragons!

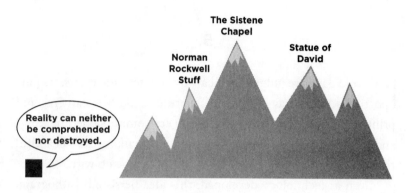

Of course, some art serves as more provocation than anything; it encourages us to do important things. It was a statue of Alexander the Great that inspired Julius Caesar to elevate his ambitions, after all.

But the *Black Square* did none of this for me. Why would people revere this thing so much?

And, you may be asking yourself at this point, what role could a guy like Malevich possibly play in our exploration of Dream Teams?

4.

I returned to the *Black Square* in Tretyakov Gallery for another look.

It didn't help. The *Black Square* was still a black square.

But after watching a few people ignore it, a college student with a punk rock haircut exuberantly walked up and took a photo of it.

"Do you like it?" I asked her.

"Of course!" she replied in a thick Russian accent.

"You are the first person I have seen be interested in this painting," I told her.

She smiled. "That is because I know the story."

5.

I n the old days, we judged visual art by how realistic it was. Its purpose was to portray reality—to capture it like the cameras and printers that didn't yet exist. Artists were commissioned by kings and wealthy patrons to make paintings and sculptures of beautiful things, using whatever materials they could come up with.

Even as technology developed, this idea persisted. Lithograph artists and printers were deemed good and effective if their output looked realistic. And though some artists eventually started exploring distortions of reality—art like Picasso's that took life and twisted it to emphasize one thing or another—they were all judged by their ability to *portray* reality and beauty.

At a certain point, however, our idea of visual art's value shifted. In the 1920s, the Bauhaus school in Germany became famous for its pioneering influence on what we know today as "graphic design," which in turn has influenced everything from advertising to the apps in our pockets. Graphic design is about more than portrayal; it is "visual communication." It has become an artistic language that helps us convey messages and persuade people in ways that words alone don't.* Without graphic design we wouldn't have websites, movie posters, or *Adventure Time* GIFs.

And what many modern website users, movie watchers, and Finn and Jake fans don't know is that the school that helped create this new artistic language owes its origins to the communists.

Two years before Bauhaus launched, Vladimir Lenin and the

---

*As the renowned graphic designer Jacqueline Casey of MIT once put it, "My job is to stop anyone I can with an arresting or puzzling image, and entice the viewer to read the message."

Bolsheviks overthrew the Russian government. They were a minority group, and in order to stay in power they needed to persuade the Russian masses of their way of thinking. So they did something clever. They hired local artists to make dramatic, impactful propaganda posters to be spread throughout Russian cities.

Many of these artists happened to belong to a new group called constructivists. They favored bold shapes and colors—mostly black and red—and symbolism over realistic portraits. A lot of it looks like cutouts of construction paper arranged on top of each other.

For example, one of the leading propaganda artists, Lazar "El" Lissitzky, created a constructivist poster of a big red triangle breaking into a white circle, called "Beat the Whites with the Red Wedge," to symbolize socialism defeating anti-communists. Lenin's followers spread this sort of thing everywhere. It wasn't "art" in the sense that people were used to, but it got the Bolsheviks' message across, powerfully.

Lissitzky had an unusual perspective on art for his time; he believed that it could serve as the vehicle for a message. And that meant art could be detached from reality and still be valuable, perhaps even more valuable than just a pretty picture. "The space must be a kind of showcase, a stage, on which the pictures make their appearance as actors in a drama (or comedy)," Lissitzky explained. "It should not imitate a living space."

The propaganda campaigns of constructivist-based art were extremely effective. Communism solidified, despite its initial minority support. But after it did so, Russia's leadership began to see artists and their ability to persuade as a threat to its control. It clamped down on the art community, and many of Lissitzky's colleagues began fleeing to Europe.

"The artists went west because of Stalin," a curator explained to me at Tretyakov. Russian art was already heavily influencing Bauhaus and other places, but after communism won and Stalin began bulldozing art that he didn't like,* she said, "The Russian avant-garde *became* European art culture."

Obviously, many things have influenced the history of graphic design. But crudely, we can say that modern graphic design came through Bauhaus, which was inspired by Russian constructivism, which was pioneered by El Lissitzky.

And why is that important? Because it turns out that El Lissitzky was the prize student of Kazimir Malevich.

Whereas Malevich's spiritual search for the "zero point of art" resulted in some not very pretty paintings, it opened the door for people like Lissitzky to use art in a new way. As the Tretyakov Gallery explains, "Suprematism totally released painting from its function of portrayal." Lissitzky passed through this door and made something exciting.

To most people, the *Black Square* itself wasn't more than a black square. But between that square of nothing and what the rest of the world called art, we discovered a mountain peak nobody had ever seen.

The *Black Square*, in other words, was useful after all. It expanded the art world's range of possibilities.

The story of the *Black Square* teaches us something counterintuitive about cognitive diversity. It teaches us that sometimes bad ideas can be useful, if anything, because a bad idea can be very good at pointing us in a new direction.

The scientific term for this is "error-allowing heuristics." The idea, as our friend Dr. Page explains, is that "sometimes, a new solution of lower value can point the way to a better solution."

This is important enough to say twice. *Sometimes a solution of lower value can point the way to a better solution.*

There's a subtlety to this idea that's also important. You'll remember that in our chapter about provocateurs, we discovered how certain collaborators can force us into The Zone when we're stuck. The *Black Square* did not exactly do this. Nobody was provoked to meaningful action because of Malevich's fringe suprematism thing. Many people didn't like it. But the *Black Square* didn't force anyone's hand.

Instead, it was when someone willingly paid attention to Malevich's crazy ideas that new possibilities opened up and progress was made.

Do you see the difference? Provocation spurs us to action; it shows us something we can't unsee. We might call what happened with Lissitzky and Malevich "cognitive expansion." It happens when we look beyond our normal frame and decide to consider new perspectives and heuristics in our process. It happens when we are curious.

In essence, cognitive expansion happens when we add cognitively diverse people to our team and pay attention to them. And it turns out that the more divergent our perspectives, the more potentially interesting the mountain range between us.

We might say that Malevich was an important member of the "team" that created graphic design, even though his ideas were bizarre and not very useful on their own. Lissitzky was curious enough to seriously explore Malevich's thinking. And this made all the difference.

Some people surely thought that Coach Tarasov was unusual for making his young hockey players learn dance and karate moves. And perhaps he was. But the Red Army invented a new way of playing the game because of it. He developed a culture of curiosity on his team—where everyone looked around the world for anything that could help them with hockey.

"Curiosity in a way [is] where some situation presents itself to you and it just doesn't make any sense," Keith Yamashita tells us. By definition it's a willingness to explore things that might not be useful. But curiosity is considered a virtue because this act of exploration is often useful regardless.

A series of research studies from the University of Leuven in Belgium shows us just how far this idea can stretch.

The Belgian researchers organized several group brainstorming sessions, with eight people each. Participants were put in rooms together and asked to come up with ideas for either mobile phone games or for a mobile payment app. They were then guided through the brainstorming activity by a moderator, who told them to write down, discuss, and sketch out as many good ideas as they could come up with.

Then came the twist. In the different sessions, the researchers added various "inspirational material" to get things going. Sometimes the inspiration was straightforward, like an idea for a prepaid credit card to use with the app. The researchers would show this idea to the group as an example, then ask them to come up with more ideas.

Other times, the researchers showed the group bad ideas. One was a bracelet that physically injures you if you spend too much money on the mobile app. This was not an idea that would ever get approved by a company—or a court of law.

Other times, the researchers included wacky characters in the group exercise. One, for example, was a washed-up actor named Patrik who had been abandoned by his wife and kids. "His best friend is his clever, but lazy dog that has the bad habit of urinating on Patrik's rug," the researchers explained. "Patrik currently has a part-time job as a private detective, providing him the income he needs to buy cheap cigars and brandy."

Here's the surprising thing. Remember how we mentioned earlier that brainstorming groups almost always produce worse ideas than their individual members will alone? Well, when the brainstorm groups in the Belgium study were given bad ideas like the injury brace-let, or crazy "collaborators" like Patrik, they came up with better ideas than they would have otherwise—together or alone.

Like the *Black Square*, the bad ideas helped point them toward ideas that they wouldn't have considered before.

In our provocation chapter, we learned about Dr. Charlan Nemeth's work on how dissent helps groups think harder about problems together. Groups with direct idea conflict are more or less forced to think more critically, to confront their issues.

But her research goes further than that. In various studies, she's been able to show that adding obviously bad ideas and viewpoints to a group's deliberation process tends to lead to better ideas, too. "The benefits of minority viewpoints do *not* depend on the 'truth' of the minority position," she writes.

Whether Malevich's spiritual suprematism thing is real or not doesn't matter if the process of considering it leads us to invent the field of graphic design.

Another key reason the Belgian studies with Patrik worked so well has to do with organizational silence. Often we have ideas in our brains that we consciously or subconsciously suppress because they fall outside what our group might deem normal. The brainstorm exercises that inject bad ideas, in a nutshell, increase the odds that we'll break our silence with an idea that would normally feel unsafe to express, because someone has already expressed something even more far out.*

This should remind us a bit of what we learned about our female police officers. If you recall, we saw that the perspective of a police officer who is not in the majority—in the case of an all-male squad, an officer who is not a man†—is often useful to a group that has been solving problems the same way for a long time. What Dr. Nemeth's research shows is that even if a minority perspective happens to be wrong, it can still help the group find better ideas as long as the group is willing to pay attention.

And this is the lesson, it turns out, all those news trucks would have learned if they had stuck around Winooski a little bit longer.

6.

The last thing the world heard about Winooski after President Carter ordered the kibosh on Mark Tigan's dome . . . was nothing.

The news correspondents drove back home. The bags of mail

---

*A study by Northwestern professor Leigh Thompson reached a similar conclusion when brainstorming participants were encouraged to share embarrassing stories about themselves before the idea session. "We found that the 'embarrassment' teams generated 26% more ideas spanning 15% more use categories than their counterparts," she writes. Sharing a candid, far-out story about yourself, she said, "led to greater creativity."

†Though studies have shown that other factors like age and sexual orientation produce similar effects.

from dome lovers stopped coming. The First International Dome Symposium became the last International Dome Symposium. The only thing left of the Winooski Dome was the occasional aside in a magazine story or blog post saying, "Remember the time those crazy Vermonters wanted to build that crazy dome?"

But it turns out that when we dig a little deeper, we learn something even crazier:

That dome that was never built helped save Winooski.

When HUD assistant secretary Embry called Tigan to relay the bad news that the dome was through, he called with another proposal.

"We can't give you the grant for the dome," Embry told him. But he knew about Burlington's proposal to build a hydroelectric plant on the river. What if he gave some federal funding to Winooski to build a hydro plant on a different part of the river that could power the area without ruining Winooski's downtown?

The enthusiasm around the dome—inventors and politicians flying in to talk about it—had ignited the town and its supporters, key among them Embry. "It demonstrated that we're willing to try things outside the box," Tigan said. With his dome, Tigan was looking at Winooski's challenges from far outside the normal range of solutions on Problem Mountain. He was so far out, in fact, that when people looked in his direction—when they started considering his far-fetched plan—it became easier for them to consider other mountain peaks hiding in the fog, from a hydroelectric plant downstream to various other projects. The dome had sparked their curiosity.

"Maybe it's not a vision of the dome, but it's a vision that these mills could be rehabbed. It's a vision that we could fill an industrial park," Tigan said. Ideas that had before gone unconsidered were not so easily dismissed anymore. "All of the sudden we were sledding downhill."

They built the hydroelectric plant, which helped Winooski save on its heating costs without ruining downtown or causing a war with Burlington. They used some of the HUD funding to convert the old factories into energy-efficient office spaces that helped attract local businesses to the town. Tigan took a bus full of townspeople up to Montreal to tell small businesses there about how great and inexpensive the new Winooski was and convinced several to open up shop there.

Even though the dome was a rather extreme—we might even say awful—idea, it ended up being useful after all. Considering such a radical idea opened Winooski and its supporters (like HUD) up to considering more workable solutions to its problems that might not have happened otherwise.

Over the course of the next couple years, unemployment in Winooski went from 15 percent to 7 percent.

And when Mark Tigan left in 1982 for his next job in Santa Monica, Winooski named a street after him.

7.

Allegedly, when Albert Einstein was asked the difference between him and the average person, he replied that the average person would stop searching for a needle in a haystack once she or he found one. Einstein, on the other hand, would keep looking through the entire haystack for all possible needles.

On the face of it, this seems like a waste of time. Why would someone ever do that? And yet, as Einstein kept marching relentlessly up and down the Problem Mountain of physics, he found a combination of perspectives that gave us the groundbreaking theory of relativity—and more.

It's often hard to recognize great perspectives even when they're in front of us, because genius and insanity often look so alike. The record companies, for example, initially rejected the Beatles amid the slew of other musicians vying for their attention. The telephone, radio, automobile, and television were each dismissed as dumb ideas by the investors of their days. Many of our most successful modern companies—from Apple to Airbnb—seemed like bad ideas in the beginning.

This leads us to back to the question we started this chapter with: How do we sort useful cognitive diversity from the useless without accidentally discounting the Einsteins, the Beatles, and the other voices we need to become better?

And as we've learned, it turns out that that's the wrong question! The lesson is that Dream Teams don't try to figure out which perspectives to ignore. They realize that if they are going to maximize the chances of making progress, the important thing is to not ignore any perspective, no matter how weird it seems.

■

Mark Tigan still likes radical ideas. He spent his career using them to get stuffy city council members to stretch their minds.

Like Soviet national team captain Valery Vasiliev—who blurred many lines on the hockey rink, doing things like getting purposely ejected from games while taking out opposing players*—Tigan played at the margins of the "rules" or conventions of his profession.

---

*In the book *The Captain Class*, *WSJ* editor Sam Walker shows persuasive evidence that the greatest sports teams of all time each had team captains who habitually pushed boundaries of rule and convention. From the 1980s and early '90s Detroit "Bad Boys" Pistons to the 1990s Cuban Olympic women's volleyball team, the best sports dynasties had team members who trekked to the edge of the mountain range.

And this helped him to expand the possibilities for the teams he worked with.

With Tigan's help, Winooski ended up securing the second-most federal funding per capita of any town in America at the time. After Winooski, Tigan went on to redevelop Santa Monica's waterfront and build a famous shopping mall. Eventually he became one of the most successful community planners in America, and HUD hired him to write its books on economic development.

When I called him up in his late sixties, he was teaching college in Massachusetts. He told me that he was still convinced that Winooski could have gotten some version of his dome to work. But more important, he said, was that they considered it. That's been his philosophy ever since. "There will be mistakes," he said. "We'll go down some wrong alleys, but I have a stomach for it, and if the organization does, too, then we'll get something done."

Seemingly bad ideas like the *Black Square* or the Winooski Dome aren't always going to end up pointing us toward useful things. But Malevich and Tigan show us just how important it is for us to seriously consider perspectives outside our norm. That's how regular teams become Dream Teams.

Now the question is, how do we get wild cards like them—or anyone, for that matter—to join our teams in the first place?

SIX*

WELCOME TO PIRATELAND

"We won the tug-of-war against the truck!"

1.

General Andrew Jackson was fresh off his latest massacre when he received the order to lead an army of pirates, whores, Choctaws, and black guys to save America from destruction.

I was excited to write that sentence. But let's back up.

It had been more than a decade since George Washington stepped down as the first president of the United States. The new country was lurching forward, collecting immigrants, and gobbling up land to the west. War wounds were healing. Factories were opening. A nation was taking shape.

Around this time, King George III of Britain and his son 4G decided to pay themselves back for some of their wartime losses over the years. Ships suddenly appeared off US coasts and began harassing American vessels. They seized cargos and conscripted sailors into the British navy by force.

---

*(To be read with a French accent.)

To retaliate, President Thomas Jefferson decided to ban all imports and exports to and from the United States.

This immediately destroyed the economy. Northern states freaked out and threatened to secede. The Southern states' cotton and tobacco rotted on their wharfs. People began to starve. Britain was fine.

As historian Winston Groom put it, this plan "would still rank near the very top of 'stupid and shortsighted legislation' were such an analytic list ever kept."* To save money, Jefferson then shrank the military.

This proved to be a bad plan when the British started stirring up American Indians to wreak havoc on frontier towns and the British kept on hijacking boats.

Then James Madison became president, and Congress declared war on the British. This, too, backfired. King George invaded Washington, burned down the White House, and pillaged cities from Virginia to Maryland. Northern states panicked. Americans for and against the war began infighting. Democratic-Republicans torched Federalist newspapers. Et cetera.

And the British realized that all this chaos presented them with a unique opportunity. With their superior military, the British reckoned they could reclaim America as a colony.

With the east coast in shambles, all the British had to do was head to the Caribbean, sail up the Mississippi, and in the words of one captain, "shove the Americans into the Atlantic Ocean." Surrounded, America would either surrender or vote to rejoin Great Britain.

---

*How Thomas Jefferson has gone down in history with such a great reputation can only be explained by the job he did in the revolution *before* his presidency. Or maybe it was just that Jefferson looked good in comparison to his vice president, Aaron Burr, the man best known for killing Alexander Hamilton. Around this time, Burr was hatching a scheme to steal some land, kick the Spanish out of Mexico, and set himself up as the ruler of a new country.

The only thing standing in the way of this plan was a raucous, booming port city in Louisiana called New Orleans.

Recently acquired from Napoleon as part of the Louisiana Purchase, New Orleans was a gateway to the Mississippi and a haven for immigration and debauchery. It was home to a mix of Creoles (local-borns of Spanish or French descent), frontiersmen, free people of color, and newcomers from around the world.

While the rest of the country starved from the import ban, New Orleans was a nonstop party. This was due in large part to a couple of local heroes: the pirate brothers Jean and Pierre Laffite.

Jean was six-foot, dark-haired, and sexy. Far from the modern peg-leg-and-parrot caricature, he was a fancy dresser who spoke elegant Spanish, English, and Italian (with a *très charmant* French accent, of course). Jean resisted the term "pirate," preferring "captain" or "privateer." His older brother Pierre ran the New Orleans blacksmith shop that served as their smuggling front. Their older brother Dominique You sailed a fleet of ships around the Caribbean looking like a straight-up pirate—striped pantaloons and all. The Laffites raided foreign ships in the Gulf and trafficked in fine silks, lace, Moroccan rugs and leather, furniture, ornate silver and china, crystal, tapestries, whiskey, rum, wine, and more.

These were complicated fellows.

In the early nineteenth century, hijacking someone else's boat was legal if your country was at war with their country. Cleverly, the Laffites sailed under letters of marque—a sort of mercenary license-to-kill—granted by the city-state of Cartagena, which conveniently happened to be at war with everybody. This way they could "legally" plunder the Spanish—and everyone else.

Importing and selling said plunder in the United States, however, was illegal—even before Jefferson's import ban. So the Laffites had set up camp on a couple of swampy islands in Barataria Bay, south of New Orleans. There they would take in ships with plunder, load their goods on rowboats, and sneak them into the city through the bayous.

The city of New Orleans left Barataria alone. So long as it let the Laffites have their little Pirateland, the city would never run out of rum.

But Jean was stockpiling gunpowder and cannonballs anyway, just in case they ever came for him.

2.

We've spent much of this book building a case for what Hollywood likes to call "the ragtag group of misfits." Though it may not always be visible on the surface, Dream Teams, we've seen, are reactors full of different kinds of particles crashing together. In this chapter we're going to explore what it takes to collect the kinds of (potentially volatile) contributors a Dream Team needs. As I said earlier, major progress requires major numbers of people. And that often means putting together coalitions—teams of teams.

In the next several pages, we'll discover how a few of our common ideas about team unity are backward. A close look at what unfolded between the United States and Britain after declaring war in 1812 will help us to see what's wrong.

As the English navy started planning its invasion of New Orleans, British colonel Edward Nicholls made a secret trip to Barataria. He had parked an armada of ships off the coast of Jamaica. Still fresh from a signal victory over Napoleon, Nicholls & Co. came with 20,000 troops, plus another 2,700 sailing close behind.

But getting to New Orleans would take tricky navigation against the twisting current of the Mississippi. To get their slow-moving ships upstream to New Orleans, they would need to disable the city's outer defenses via a ground invasion. And this meant finding a good way for tens of thousands of soldiers to get through a maze of swamps.

Nicholls offered Jean Laffite the modern-day equivalent of more than $2 million to guide them through the swamp.

Laffite agreed. He told them (likely while stroking the upturned curls of his mustache) that he would need two weeks to get his affairs in order. Pleased, Nicholls's men returned to the fleet to make preparations.

And Laffite promptly went to the Louisiana government and told them of the Brits' plan, the details of which he had learned after getting the British envoy drunk off smuggled rum.

Ironically, the state of Louisiana was currently trying to get rid of the pirate brothers. Since New Orleans hadn't been doing anything to stop them, Governor William Claiborne had recently offered a $500 reward for "the capture and delivery of Jean Laffite."

Cocky (and sexy) as ever, Jean Laffite had countered by posting handbills across the city declaring an even larger reward for the capture and delivery of Governor Claiborne. The state retaliated by sending a schooner of war to clear out Barataria. At the same time Laffite was double-crossing the British, the pirates were busy hiding all their cannons and treasure in the swamp.

Why the pirates would help the government, their enemy, over the British, was a curious matter. But New Orleans was home, and Laffite loved America—if not its politicians.*

Upon learning of Colonel Nicholls's plan, the US government freaked out. America had never planned to defend the Mississippi, let alone with what few ill-equipped soldiers there were in the New

---

*Furthermore, in the midst of all this, Pierre Laffite had been locked up on smuggling charges. But after Jean exposed the British scheme to the state legislature, Pierre "mysteriously" escaped. Criminal prosecutions against the Baratarians were quickly dropped. And once Pierre was released, the Laffites did not run away. . . .

Orleans area. Lacking a modern-day national military, the best President Madison could do was call up a lawyer-cum-militia commander from Tennessee who was known for waging war with native tribes—Andrew Jackson—and say, essentially, "Do what you can."

Jackson was also a complicated character. He was known for his fiery temper, his stubbornness, and his unwillingness to compromise what he thought was right. These traits did not always square up.

For example, one time he nearly killed the Tennessee state governor in a duel over an insult. Another time he (a) got shot in the arm, after (b) trying to horsewhip some dude, who (c) had gotten mad when Jackson's friend, (d) had shot that guy's friend in the butt.*

It was not long after this that Jackson received the panicky request from Washington that he go to New Orleans.

Jackson showed up in the city with a bad case of dysentery and his arm in a sling. Knowing what the British soldiers had done to villagers in Maryland, the people of New Orleans were understandably terrified. The city's entire defense consisted of a makeshift battalion of 287 local lawyers and businessmen, two regiments of poorly equipped Louisiana State Militia, a feisty contingent of local whores who'd volunteered for sewing and ammo duty, and 107 cavalry. There was also a militia battalion of 210 freemen of color in the area. They had not been paid in a while, but Jackson persuaded them to join. To round out the army, Jackson brought with him a crew of 1,800 unshaven Tennessee volunteers with hatchets and hunting rifles called "dirty shirts."

This was the team that had to take on some 20,000 trained Britons. None of these motley volunteers had ever fought together, and

---

*Let's go over that again so the sequence is clear: A guy mooned Jackson's buddy. So Jackson's buddy shot the guy in his exposed rear. And when the butt-shot guy's friend got mad about this, Jackson tried to horsewhip said friend. The mad friend then defended himself by shooting Jackson. In the arm. Simple as that.

few had ever seen a real battle. At stake: their lives, their city, and the future of the United States of America.

Jackson put New Orleans under martial law and gave a speech. He ordered the citizens to "cease all differences and divisions" and unite with him to defend the city. The townspeople cheered. The ragtag army began digging a moat and rampart in front of the city.

But this was insufficient, and Jackson knew it.

Two additional groups of fighters were available, he learned. One was a crew of sixty-two Choctaw braves. The other, to his dismay, was a gang of criminals who happened to own a lot of cannons: the Baratarians.

Jackson hated the French. He hated the Creoles. He hated criminals. As a slave owner and Creek War vet, Jackson was hardly on the right side of history when it came to black people or American Indians. And Jackson really, really hated pirates.

But he hated the British more.*

Jean Laffite's lawyer—a man named Edward Livingston†— brokered a meeting between the general and his client. Jackson was charmed by the mustachioed privateer. In addition to cannons, Laffite had stockpiled flints, gunpowder, rifles, and pistols. Jackson made his case for setting aside differences to save the city, and Laffite joined up as the army's co-strategist.

The Choctaws joined up as well, and the New Orleans defense force became the most diverse group of soldiers ever to fight together in the history of America. They were still outnumbered at least six to one.

The British ferried their army through the bayous and camped a

---

*They had left him an orphan in the Revolutionary War. His mother died of cholera while tending wounded aboard a British ship. He wholeheartedly loathed the British, who dared try to take his home away once again, with, as Theodore Roosevelt would put it, "an implacable fury that was absolutely devoid of fear."

†Basically the Saul Goodman of the 1810s.

few miles south of New Orleans, intending to attack Jackson's ramparts by day. During the night, however, the Baratarians floated a ship downriver with the lights off and parked across from the British camp. The British noticed, hailed, fired some warning shots at it, then decided it must be a fisherman or something. Tired from rowing through the swamp all day, they went to bed.

Suddenly the gun ports snapped open, and the pirates opened fire on the camp.

This was not how wars were fought. The British were used to "civilized" warfare, where smartly dressed soldiers marched in tight formations, looked their enemies in the eyes, and won through strength and honor.

Pirates don't believe in any of that crap. They bombarded the British camp all night. When they ran out of cannonballs, they put chains and kitchenware in the guns, dismembering everything in range.

The British hadn't anticipated needing artillery in this battle. The winds wouldn't allow them to bring their own ships upriver for weeks. It would take days to bring ground cannons through the swamps to counterattack the ship. So the army dug trenches, hid in the mud, and waited.

Meanwhile, the Choctaws started sneaking around the swamp and tomahawking British sentries. They picked off anyone who happened to walk into the woods to pee or whose tent was too far away from the main camp. At the same time, the Dirty Shirts used their hunting rifles to assassinate pickets from afar.

The British officers thought it terribly unchivalrous. This was how Indian skirmishes were fought, they said, not noble wars! Nicholls sent a messenger under a flag of truce to request that they stop this nonsense and fight like gentlemen. Jackson received the envoy and sent him back with a cordial request that the invading colonel go fuck himself.

The British finally managed to drag their artillery through the swamp. They blew up the Baratarians' boat. But by this time the pirates had brought an even bigger ship downriver—one with more range than the British artillery. The cannonade continued.

Jackson issued whiskey to all his soldiers and prepared for the all-out charge he knew was coming. The only way the British could avoid the pirates' harassing fire was to go ahead and storm Jackson's line with brute force.

By the time the British finally charged, Jackson had dug a giant moat and thrown up dirt ramparts several feet high. Following Laffite's advice, he'd extended the rampart a half mile into the swamp, where it turns out the British were planning to focus their assault. Behind the wall he placed the Dirty Shirt riflemen and Baratarian cannoneers, led by Jean's brother Dominique You.

The final attack came on Sunday morning, January 8, 1815. As the endless horde of British soldiers charged, the motley crew of American defenders opened fire. There was so much smoke that they had to periodically stop shooting and let the air clear so the Dirty Shirts could aim their sharpshooter guns. These long-barreled frontier rifles proved particularly effective in picking off British officers, who made crisp targets in their bright coats and tall hats. Again, this was not cool. But it worked. Meanwhile, a single shell from the pirate artillery could kill fifteen men at a time. The British watched their own cannons sink into the mud.

When the dust cleared, the British had suffered 3,750 casualties. The Americans had only 333.

This was going to be too hard, the British decided. They packed their things and made the sad trek back through the swamp, back to their boats.

The British ships went home. And New Orleans threw a party.*

---

* *Laissez les bon temps rouler, n'est-ce pas?*

The Battle of New Orleans went down in history as one of the most brilliant feats of military strategy ever. The outcome was due in large part to overconfidence on the part of Colonel Nicholls and his fellows. Yet despicable as he often was, General Jackson deserves some applause as well. Working with people he typically despised, he turned a band of misfits into a Dream Team. In our friend Keith Yamashita's parlance, Jackson "cast" the perfect team for the job.

As you'll undoubtedly recognize by now, the real story of this victory is not about Jackson's leadership. It's the thing we've been talking about from the beginning. It was not raw intelligence or skill that won the battle. What ultimately saved the day was an array of disparate fighting heuristics, and diverse perspectives.

In other words, if not for the "misfit" part of Jackson's band of misfits, the United States might today have the Queen on its fiver.*

The Dirty Shirts' hunting rifles could shoot farther and straighter than any British soldier's could. They couldn't load their guns nearly as fast, but given the logistics of the battle, the Tennesseans didn't have to. The Choctaws destroyed the morale of the British troops (not to mention their scouting eyes and ears) with their nighttime assassinations. And without the Baratarians' cannon work or Laf-

---

*The Treaty of Ghent, which ended the War of 1812, was signed days before the first shots were fired at the Battle of New Orleans, but it took a month for word to arrive. Had Nicholls taken New Orleans and continued up the Mississippi, many speculate that the treaty would not have held. At the very least, it's likely that the pattern of sacking and raping that British soldiers effectuated up and down the east coast would have continued here. But no one can know for sure what would have happened.

fite's strategic advice, Jackson was certain his line would have fallen to the enemy.

The legend of this battle propelled Jackson into national fame. He got into politics and became the seventh president of the United States. Edward Livingston became his secretary of state.

And Jean Laffite, no longer a wanted man, became a local celebrity. He started going to fancy parties, where he went from stealing boats to stealing something he liked even more: the hearts of New Orleans' beautiful married ladies.

3.

We've talked a lot about the need for different heuristics and perspectives to make progress together. We've talked about how we need to make cognitive friction to make those differences matter. And we've discussed how Dream Teams depressurize tension, leverage provocation, and open themselves to wild-card ideas to find solutions that others can't.

Jackson and his misfit army are a classic example of a Dream Team that did all of this. But their story also points us to an important question we need answered: How do Dream Teams need to be united, not different?

Jackson and Laffite were nothing alike. Yet their heads combined to form a defense strategy that turned overwhelming odds into ten-to-one casualties in their favor. The Choctaws and the Tennesseans were outright enemies. Working together they were unstoppable. The battalion of free blacks built ramparts and shot rifles alongside slave owners whom they had every right to hate. The Baratarians manned cannons with the very soldiers who'd been sent by the governor to break up their colony. And yet they formed an incredible coalition.

We see from this that we don't need to be alike to be united. We don't even need to like each other. We just need a good-enough common cause we all want more than anything else—in this case a collective enemy and the collective mission of saving the city.

Psychologists call this a "superordinate goal."

A superordinate goal isn't just a common goal. It's one that takes precedence over all others. You'd like for America to remain a free country more than you'd like $2 million, for example. These are the kinds of goals that get us to overcome our usual hang-ups about working together.

History shows time and time again that superordinate goals have the power to unite even the most different of people.

The United States and the Baratarians were enemies. Jackson was not a tolerant guy. The black soldiers had a limited sort of freedom amid a society that treated them as subhumans and property. The Choctaws had every reason to say, "You deserve it," were the British to beat up the Americans.

But as the old Sanskrit proverb summed it up more than two thousand years ago, these hostile parties realized that "the enemy of my enemy is my friend." Everyone's desire to keep their home superseded their desire for British gold, or their desire to get revenge for fights and slights of the past. Their superordinate goal brought them together.

It looks like the answer to our question about becoming a united group is simple. No matter how different we are, if we develop a superordinate goal, then we can work together without falling apart.

Except for one little problem. It's what happened to Jean Laffite after the Battle of New Orleans was over.

4.

On February 6, 1815, President James Madison pardoned the Laffites and their men for any crimes they may have committed before the war. The Baratarians had donated their weapons to the cause of saving America, and they had fought bravely.

But the Louisiana government had in the meantime decided to seize the Baratarians' stuff. All the silks and rum and furniture and fine goods that they'd spent years stockpiling—and which Madison had essentially promised not to ask where it came from—all ended up locked in Governor Claiborne's warehouses.

Jean Laffite sued. The case went all the way to the Supreme Court. Laffite insisted that he had never actually engaged in piracy. He was technically a Cartagenan privateer, which made his plundering in international waters legal as far as US courts were concerned. Ironically, the governor taking Laffite's goods amounted to a more clear-cut theft.

But the state of Louisiana turned on Laffite. Now that the existential threat was over and American shipping was back in business, they didn't need the Baratarians. Claiborne kept Jean Laffite's stuff and made him a wanted man again.

So the Laffites took their boats and sailed to Galveston, an island off the coast of Texas, where they set up a new Pirateland.

After the battle, Jackson's loyalties dissolved as well.* He began quarreling with the government almost immediately. Jackson had imprisoned a meddlesome federal judge when he put New Orleans

---

*Few who worked with Jackson seemed to really like him when he wasn't rallying an army toward a superordinate goal. He was a man of strange and harsh standards. Later as president he would publicly bad-mouth his own vice president and send thousands of American Indians marching west, many to their deaths.

under martial law. Now that the civilian government was back in control, the judge was suing Jackson for wrongful imprisonment.

Furthermore, days after the battle, Jackson publicly executed six volunteer civilian soldiers who had asked to go home. Until the official peace treaty was signed, Jackson was still in command under martial law. These men's three-month contract was up, but Jackson commanded them to stay. When they tried to go home anyway, he had them shot in front of everyone in the city to make a point. One of them was a Baptist preacher with nine children at home. He begged for mercy, and Jackson gave him none.*

In his official reports, Jackson left out the part where the pirates supplied the gunpowder, flints, and cannons that made victory possible. He gave Jean Laffite a brief commendation but downplayed his strategic role in saving the city. Jackson's personal code prohibited him from giving criminals like them credit even when it was due.

Laffite never forgave Jackson for that. The Baratarians had different ideas around fairness and equality than Jackson did.

It turns out that superordinate goals, for all their rallying power, can be fleeting. Once the goal is met or changes, parties have little reason to help each other. Thus, a relationship built on a mutual enemy often only lasts as long as the enemy does. We often go right back to fighting each other afterward.

In the Battle of New Orleans, the intentions of a whole bunch of different people aligned for a period of time. But when the goal was achieved, there was no glue to hold them together.

A hundred and twenty-five years after the Battle of New Orleans, a common enemy brought Americans and Britons together

---

*Citizens were justifiably outraged. But worse, as it turned out, the peace treaty had been ratified five days before the execution. Messengers had simply not yet arrived from Washington. This nearly cost Jackson the presidency when it came out in the national press years later. It should have.

in a similar way. The superordinate goal of stopping Adolf Hitler brought them, along with Communist Russia, together. After they defeated the Nazis, the United States and Russia went back to distrusting each other. But something interesting happened between America and Britain. They solidified a long-term alliance. The two countries had been growing more friendly over the years, and coming together to beat the Nazis cinched the relationship.

This was not because they shared a language and ethnicity (Brits were oft dismissive of American speech, and more Americans were of non-British descent than otherwise). Many historians argue that it was because the two countries had something in common that they didn't with Russia: a strong set of shared values.

America and Britain for the most part believed in similar principles of government, theology, and ethics. When the superordinate goal of stopping Hitler forced the United States and England to work together, they realized that they had a lot in common, and stuck together.

We see this happen in business all the time. Researchers Jim Collins and Jerry Porras point out that successful companies often have "cultlike" values. Their employees must abide the values or find someplace else to work. "Such cult-like atmospheres are highly productive and filled with enthusiasm," writes Dr. Nemeth, whom we met earlier. Companies who talk about shared values a lot will tend to unify their people quickly and effectively. Research shows that they tend to have low turnover and relatively stable businesses.

As we've seen, shared goals help us come together. But what keeps us from falling apart after the existential threat is over? It's not our shared goals. It's our shared beliefs.

Except, it turns out that this, too, isn't quite right. In fact, it can be a huge problem.

One of the saddest parts of the Battle of New Orleans is what happened to the British 93rd Regiment. This group of 1,100 proud Scotsmen were each required to be over six feet tall. They looked awesome. They wore plaid tartan trousers and marched precisely to the tune of bagpipes.

They were practically boys. They'd been told by their king that if they served the crown well, they would be rewarded handsomely.

The British army was the most disciplined in the world. It had a strong culture of shared values: unflinching bravery, unquestioning loyalty, and impeccable obedience. When you received an order, you never questioned and never deviated.

The Scotsmen were among the best at adhering to these values. Until it killed them.

During the battle's final assault, the 93rd's commander was shot right after he gave an order to halt. The troops halted. And then they waited obediently for their next order, standing like statues directly in front of Jackson's rampart. They were determined to do nothing but "halt" until told otherwise.

Jackson's men blasted them to pieces. Over and over they shot their cannons at these sitting ducks, taking out six hundred men before someone finally shouted, "Retreat!"

Dr. Nemeth's research shows that strong shared cultural values in an organization, despite the stability they bring, have one big flaw. They backfire. The stricter the values, the more potential for catastrophic outcomes. "In fact," writes Dr. Nemeth, "there is evidence that the atmosphere most likely to induce creativity is one diametrically opposed to the 'cult like.'"

Shared values, she says, make us more likely to think the same, to not question the way the group thinks. They shift different perspectives toward the same perspective. This is good for keeping peace, but not for problem solving. It sucks the group out of The Zone.

Some organizations try to combat this by making "creativity" and "taking risks" values themselves. However, data show that that doesn't really work. Groups that have a lot of cultural similarity stop searching for better solutions once they have solutions that work. They think they are creative because it's a value. But, Dr. Nemeth points out, "Good intentions and great effort do not necessarily result in creativity."

And like we learn from the devastating story of those poor Scots, strong shared values often do not result in good problem solving.

Seven out of ten American employees in companies with strong values hush up when their opinions are at odds with those of their superiors, according to research by University of Southern California professor Warren Bennis. Requiring adherence to strong values, in other words, promotes organizational silence.

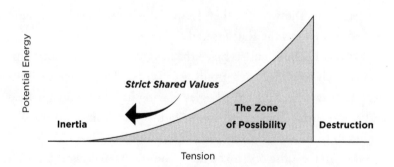

As we've learned throughout this book, Dream Teams need to have, seriously consider, and combine different perspectives. And having different perspectives often goes hand in hand with having different values.* And yet, coalitions that lack shared values, like that of Jackson and Laffite, often don't seem to last.

Are we to conclude that Dream Teams are doomed to be fleeting?

Fortunately, the answer is no. There's just a little more to the equation than simply "shared goals" or "shared values."

To unpack it, we're going to look at some other pirates. These ones just happen to be twelve years old.

5.

I n 1954, Muzafer Sherif, one of the early pioneers of social psychology, conducted a devious experiment.

He and some colleagues set up a three-week summer camp for a bunch of twelve-year-old boys from Oklahoma. The location was Robbers Cave, a famous old woodland hideout of Jesse James. Sherif put the boys into two groups of eleven. For a week, neither group knew about the other as it went about cooking and hiking and playing games in the woods. They formed their own leadership and named themselves the Rattlers and the Eagles.

Gradually, the scientists made the boys aware of each other. This immediately solidified each group against the other. When the Rattlers, for example, heard the Eagles playing baseball, they groaned and complained. They called them "bums" and "communists." The Eagles in turn referred to the Rattlers as "stinkers."†

The camp counselors stoked the animosity by making the groups

---

*Wise groups, even ones that have strong values in common, recognize the importance of allowing people to break cultural ranks in the name of progress. In Judaism, for example, you're allowed to break any rule if it's to save a life.

† Such great insults in those days!

play tug-of-war and football against each other. Soon the groups were pilfering from each other's cabins and throwing garbage at one another.

Sherif was one of the first scientists to note that group dynamics like this create what's called "perceptual distortion." He observed that just learning of the existence of a distinct group was all that was needed to foster bias. His research was the beginning of what we understand today of in-group and out-group psychology.

When perceptual distortion happens, the differences between members of the same group get minimized and even ignored. "Members of the same category seem to be more similar than they actually are and more similar than they were before they were categorized together," write psychologists Samuel Gaertner and John Dovidio. And the differences of the out-group get exaggerated and overgeneralized. "Positive behaviors and successful outcomes are more likely to be attributed to internal, stable characteristics (the personality) of in-group than out-group members," they write. "Whereas negative outcomes are more likely to be ascribed to the personalities of out-group members than of in-group members."

Sounds like a description of racism, sexism, or any other -ism, doesn't it? It is.

So it went with the Eagles and the Rattlers. Before long, the boys were walking around camp with sticks, bats, and socks filled with rocks. Fistfights and food fights broke out.

Then the camp counselors sabotaged the water supply. Nobody had anything to drink. The counselors said they suspected a leak or a clog somewhere along the pipe between camp and the water tank above it. They would need each boy's help to find it.

The boys split up along their in-group lines to go search for the kink. As the counselors planned, everyone ended up at the water tank at the top of the hill where it turned out the problem lay.

It took several boys from both groups to unclog it. Afterward, everyone was so pleased that nobody fought over who got to drink first. They still walked back to camp separately, though.

So far so good, the experimenters must have thought, stroking their mustaches like modern Jean Laffites.

Next, the counselors informed the group that they were going to rent the film *Treasure Island* for all the boys to watch. But they were fifteen dollars short. Even though a couple of Eagles had gone home and the groups were now uneven, the boys agreed to pony up an equal amount per group to get the movie for everyone. They were learning to cooperate around superordinate goals.

Then, during an expedition to the lake, the camp truck that was supposed to get the food "wouldn't start." They boys were all hungry. So they decided to use their tug-of-war rope together to pull the truck to "jump-start" it. The counselor faked the engine failure and jump start. As the truck roared to life, the boys cheered, "We won the tug-of-war against the truck!" They patted each other on the back and didn't segregate themselves in the queue for food when it arrived.

This was a turning point. The boys were starting to use the term "we" to refer to everyone instead of just their own group.

The experimenters called this "decategorization and recategorization." As the boys worked together on the shared goals, they began to get to know each other as individuals. This started breaking down their category stereotypes. The Rattlers weren't so bad, it turned out! Nor were the Eagles!

And this opened the door for the boys to start seeing both groups as part of something more important. A superordinate group.

With this, something crucial happened. Inside the superordinate group, the boys did what the researchers called "mutual differentiation." They began to recognize the strengths that individuals had— such as one boy who was good at cutting meat—and that each group had—such as different fun camp songs that they could teach each other.

This led to a "more respectful appreciation of differences between the groups." Instead of seeing their differences as problems, they saw them as potential assets for the group. With this, the boys didn't just find common goals and unique strengths, they developed respect.

By the end of the camp, the boys still defined themselves as Eagles or Rattlers, but they began to think of both groups as subgroups of a bigger group that they all belonged to. "During breakfast and lunch on the last day of camp, the seating was without regard to earlier group membership as it was on the bus ride home to Oklahoma City," the researchers noted. "The boys crowded close together toward the front of the bus as a single group singing 'Oklahoma.'"

With the Robbers Cave kids, we once again see how superordinate goals can get different people to work together. We see a little of what we learned in chapter 3, that play and humor can depressurize groups that have too much tension between them.

And we also learn from this study the importance of developing a mutual respect for our differences. We learn that to succeed, we need to break down the walls between human categories and see ourselves as part of a superordinate group.

The boys in the camp shared some values, like the idea of taking turns and fairness, but they didn't see eye to eye on everything. That didn't matter by the end. They learned to respect each other and see themselves as both Rattlers and Eagles *and* something bigger.

Andrew Jackson did not respect Jean Laffite and the Baratarians or the Choctaws or the free blacks. He didn't think of them as Americans but as outsiders, useful for his goals but not people to include in his in-group. So after the battle was over, they parted ways.

6.

There's a scene in the movie *The Rocketeer* that I loved when I was a kid. Toward the finale, the police get in a gunfight with mobsters who have been colluding with the movie's villain, Timothy Dalton. Dalton is secretly an evil Nazi. While his goons shoot at the police, he begins his escape in an enormous blimp.

As the blimp takes off, it reveals a giant Nazi flag.

When the head mobster, Eddie Valentine, sees the flag, he is caught by surprise. He looks at the cops he's been shooting at . . . then turns his Tommy Gun toward the Nazis. "I may not make an honest buck," he declares. "But I'm 100 percent American. I don't work for no two-bit Nazi." The mobsters and the police suddenly start working together.

The mobsters and the cops had different values. They had different goals. But at the crucial moment, a shared identity united them. And Valentine's superordinate goal, the success of his American in-group, became more important than the job Nazi Dalton was paying him to do.

Like we talked about earlier, the psychological purpose of in-groups is to help human beings know when they can trust each other's intentions. This helps us feel safe enough to take the risks we need to make progress. Once the mobsters and the police in *The Rocketeer* reframed their situation around the shared identity of being all-American, they were willing to turn their backs to each other's weapons without fear.

When it comes to Dream Teams, there's an important point of distinction about this kind of superordinate group trust that's worth emphasizing. Trusting in a person's ability is one thing. We don't need to be in the same group to do this. But trusting someone's intentions—as the best teams do—is quite powerful. When we trust someone's intentions, it's suddenly all right if they are different—if they believe different things, have different goals from time to time, or even if they make mistakes. With that kind of respect, we are able to have cognitive friction without things becoming personal and blowing up. We can be free to dissent or disagree or correct each other, because we start from a place of, "I know you don't mean any harm to me."

On the face of it, this chapter presents us with a paradox. Strong shared values help keep groups together, but research shows that they also promote detrimental groupthink. At the same time, in this chapter we've learned that the value of respect is paramount for disparate groups to come together as one superordinate group.

And actually, if we think back on everything we've discussed so far, we realize that each chapter of this book has made the case for values that Dream Teams need to share. In our buddy cops chapter we learned why we need to value differences. With Wu-Tang we proved the value of engaging with each other openly and candidly. Carol Vallone taught us how play can help us do that better. Nellie Bly showed us the value of inviting provocation and dissent. Mark Tigan and Malevich helped us understand the need for boundless curiosity. And this chapter has shown us why every great team has to have mutual respect.

Laying all this out makes the answer to our paradox actually pretty obvious: it's that not all values are created equal. Values that help us *include* different kinds of people and ideas are the kinds of values we want our teams to share. Values that don't have to do with inclusion are values we don't really need to have in common—and in fact, if we have too many of those other kinds of values in common, it's a sign we need to expand our circle.

Besides, when organizations talk about their "values," they're often conflating values with practices. "The customer is always right," "simplify," and "find balance" are policies and behaviors, not values. And policies and behaviors like these may be great most of the time, but when taken literally and without room for dissent, they can result in the building burning down. They may rally people together, but they restrict progress up the mountain.

We might say, in other words, that a Dream Team is like a family. Family members may not always see eye to eye. Some may not end up choosing to hold on to all the same values as they grow up. There may be a black sheep or two. But in a good family, a bond supersedes these differences. Members can come together for family rituals that bring them closer, while maintaining their individuality. And this helps develop what sports writer Bill Simmons calls "an unselfish culture."* Like the Red Army hockey players, a family member who can simultaneously belong and contribute meaningfully is liable to choose the team's success over his or her personal success.

This is the kind of team that can regroup and do what needs to be done whenever a new challenge arises. Like the Russian Five. Or Wu-Tang. Or Pinkerton's National Detective Agency.

There's one final value that makes the whole Dream Team thing work. It's a virtue that we've hinted at throughout the book, and one that the individual members of great teams need to have in order to fully harness their potential energy. And it's what we're going to spend the last two chapters of this book exploring.

---

*Our big problem with modern politics stems not from different values but from a lack of respect that comes with not seeing different values as an advantage that helps us as a group. It's exactly what George Washington warned about in his presidential farewell speech. Washington hated the idea of political parties because they divide our identity. They make it easy to forget that we're on the same side.

سبعة

WHEN MALCOLM CHANGED HIS MIND

"It forced me . . . to toss aside
some of my previous conclusions."

1.

Four-year-old Malcolm Little's earliest memory was of white supremacists burning down his house.

It was 1929. The Ku Klux Klan had recently broken the windows of his parents' home in Lansing, Michigan, threatening worse if the family didn't move out of the neighborhood. They hadn't moved. But now they did.

Instead of searching for the arsonist, the local police locked Little's father up "in case" he was the one who did it. They had nothing that resembled evidence, so the judge let him out.

Not long after, Little's father was run over by a streetcar. The police ruled his death an accident. The locals, on the other hand, said a KKK member pushed him.

Little's mom couldn't afford to feed all seven children now that Dad was gone. She cracked. By the time Little was a teenager, she was living in a mental hospital.

He told his schoolteachers that he wanted to be a lawyer. But racism stood in the way of that one, too. "You've got to be realistic about being a nigger," his English teacher told him. "A lawyer—that's no realistic goal. Why don't you plan on carpentry?"

Angry, Little dropped out of school. He went to live with his half sister in Boston, a woman who had faced several criminal prosecutions. She, too, soon ended up in a mental hospital.

He started smoking drugs. Then selling drugs. Then stealing to pay for drugs. At age nineteen, he got caught trying to fence a watch. Little went to trial for burglary.

By the time his white girlfriend sold him out from the witness box—and the judge gave him the maximum sentence because, as the prosecution put it, "you had no business with white girls"—Little decided that he hated white people. He had six to eight years to let that hate fester from inside a federal prison.

Little was surly and uncooperative for his first year in the joint. Other inmates gave him the nickname "Satan" for his foul mouth. He smuggled in drugs. When he couldn't get high the regular way, he snorted nutmeg, which has a cannabis-like effect at high concentration. He was full of hate.*

An older inmate named Bembry took Little under his wing, and convinced him that if he got educated, he might get his sentence reduced. Seeing Bembry as a father figure, Little took the advice. He started taking mail-in courses, reading books, and memorizing dictionary words. He started writing letters, and, to the guards' bemusement, he stopped cursing.

Around this time, Little began a correspondence with the leader

---

*And nutmeg.

of a tiny new religious group.* His siblings had recently joined. The group preached a mixed-up new version of Islam. It called for no pork, no booze, no extramarital sex, and other items of strict self-discipline, but mainstream Muslims refused to recognize it because of some of its new ideas and its lack of basic tenets such as believing Muhammad to be the last prophet. But Little had no way of knowing that. He was drawn by the fact that the group's leader—a man named Elijah Poole—claimed that God had taught him the truth about white people.

Thousands of years ago, Elijah's story went, everyone in the world had dark skin. Then a disturbed man named Yacub created white people as a sort of primeval science experiment. They were all devils, the leader taught. And so were their descendants today.

At first, Little found this story hard to believe. Whites had cited a similar story for centuries as justification for slavery and racism toward black people.†

Yet the more Little thought about his interactions with white people so far in his young life, the more he realized that almost every one he had met had treated him badly. He had an epiphany. They *were* devils.

Little joined the fold and was soon trying to convert other convicts. He began spending all his time studying and debating religion. He got especially good at preaching about the badness of white supremacy and the newfound truth of black supremacy.

When Little got paroled in 1952, he moved to Detroit to become

---

*Little's biographer Manning Marable and other scholars characterized the group in its early days as a "cult." By definition, every religious society built around a personality, with strict in-group rules and low tolerance for dissent, is a "cult" until it grows into something mainstream. But also, these guys were a little scary.

†One interpretation of a passage from the Old Testament (Genesis 9:25, KJV) concludes that dark skin came from a curse Noah put on his wicked grandson Canaan. In calling whites cursed, Elijah was turning this narrative on its head.

a minister. He'd been reborn. "I don't think anybody ever got more out of going to prison than I did," he said. "I have fully awakened."

With his rebirth, he got rid of the name Little.

He now called himself Malcolm X.

The group's leader, Elijah, claimed to be the infallible Messenger of Allah. He claimed to have seen God and been given the duty of becoming supreme leader of the "Lost-Found Nation of Islam." Elijah's Nation required strict obedience and donations from his four hundred followers.

X had developed impressive speaking skills from debating in prison. The history of Yacub was a great attention getter, he learned. But the more he preached, the more he emphasized another message that underpinned the religion, and the growing Black Muslim movement in general: that the black man deserved self-respect.

This message resonated with poor African American males especially. It gave many downtrodden black men hope they desperately deserved.

Unfortunately, the Nation of Islam's doctrine at the time dovetailed this message with militant violence and a disdain for anyone who preached racial integration. It was also pretty sexist. This put the group at odds with the growing civil rights movement in the Southern United States.

But it gave NOI followers hope nonetheless. X's sermons for this newfangled brand of Islam soon attracted larger crowds than Messenger Elijah's.

With this knack for preaching, X helped grow the NOI's membership by a thousand people in a year. Soon he was attracting a thousand a month. He set up a Boston chapter, then New York and Philadelphia chapters. Before he knew it, he was giving speeches to crowds of four thousand at a time.

Elijah's bank account grew. He bought a mansion in Chicago, then another in Arizona.

The little church was becoming a full-fledged religion, and also a paramilitary group. Suddenly X was overseeing legions of volunteer enforcers. They trained in karate and would brutally beat members who disobeyed Elijah.

Things were getting a little out of hand. The Nation of Islam wanted their own country, a few states that could break off from the United States. Or ideally some territory in Africa they could run themselves. X preached that the black man should "take matters into his own hands" and use violence against the white government to get that separation. He decried the nonviolent civil rights movement of Dr. Martin Luther King Jr. in the south, accusing King of being a puppet of the white devils. From his pulpit, X called Jews evil, Christians evil, and women weak.

While Dr. King and his colleagues pushed for equality and integration, X and the Nation of Islam pushed for the opposite. They negotiated alliances with the Ku Klux Klan and the American Nazi Party to promote the thing all three groups wanted: to keep blacks and whites far apart from each other. Unlike King and his followers, X did not believe that white people could ever stop hating black people. How could they, after all, if they were literally devils?

As X's profile grew, he had a series of public debates with Bayard Rustin, a key member of Dr. King's civil rights team, whom you may recall from our Angelic Troublemakers chapter. X and Rustin represented the edges of two schools of thought among black advocacy groups in the mid-twentieth-century struggle for rights. On the left were liberal types who argued for racial integration and even socialism—Rustin being on the fringe of this as a former communist. On the right were conservative types who argued for black business ownership and independent communities—the fringe of which advocated for a separate nation for black people entirely. The Nation of Islam's militant point of view on this was so far right, it was almost over the cliff.

In their debates, Rustin argued for nonviolent revolution. X advocated the reverse. "We are not to turn the other cheek," he said. Instead of joining the famous 1963 March on Washington for civil rights, X denounced it, saying it was a waste of time. Peaceful marches were what the "white man" wanted, he said.

When an airplane crash in Paris killed 121 white people, X called it "a very beautiful thing." He called President Kennedy "a prison warden," and American whites who supported racial integration "snakelike." When Kennedy was assassinated, Little told the press that he had it coming.

Dr. King and other civil rights activists denounced X for this. "The hatred expressed toward whites by Malcolm X is not shared," King declared. "While there is a great deal of legitimate discontent and righteous indignation in the Negro community, it has never developed into a large-scale hatred."

Black civil rights leaders backed away from X. White leaders on both sides of the political spectrum were terrified of him. The Nazi Party kept showing up to his rallies to support his separatist agenda. The FBI put him under surveillance. And angry black supremacists kept flocking to the NOI and training in guns and karate.

And then something impossible happened.

X went off the grid for a little while. When he came back, he began talking very differently.

"A man should not be judged by the color of his skin," Malcolm X declared in an interview, "but rather by his conscious behavior, by his actions."

What?

His followers were dismayed. Was this a joke? Or perhaps a ploy?

It wasn't. X clarified himself. "I believe in taking an uncompromising stand against any forms of segregation and discrimination."

Had the separatist just taken up the integration torch of the civil rights movement? Was he going to join Rustin and King?! That couldn't be right.

While his fans waited for him to say, "Just kidding!" X kept saying things like, "I believe in a society in which people can live like human beings on the basis of equality."

People on both sides were shocked. What prompted this? Where was the fiery preacher who'd taught so many to fight white supremacy with black supremacy?

He was gone. X renounced the label "Black Nationalist." He even started saying that women in his organization should have an "equal position to men." He abandoned the Nation of Islam and became a Sunni Muslim. He declared that it would take "Christians, Jews, Buddhists, Hindus, agnostics, and even atheists . . . to make the Human Family." If we wanted to make a better world for oppressed black people, he said, we all needed to work together as a team.

With this change of heart, X began writing newspaper articles with titles like "Racism: The Cancer That Is Destroying America." He told the press, "I do not advocate violence." In another surprising turnaround, he also declared, "Whoever a person wants to love, that's their business."

In interviews, X expressed remorse for many of his past views and actions. "Remember the time that white college girl came into the restaurant—the one who wanted to help the Muslims and the whites get together—and I told her there wasn't a ghost of a chance and she went away crying?" he said to a local reporter. "I've lived to regret that incident . . . I'm sorry."

Malcolm X's transformation was so complete and so upsetting to the NOI leadership that many people were not surprised to hear the news when, on the afternoon of February 21, 1965, a man stood up in the front row of the Audubon Theater in Harlem during X's speech, and pulled a shotgun out from under his coat.

2.

How does a person change deeply held views despite knowing that it could be the death of him? What prevents so many of us from doing the same with much lower stakes?

This is perhaps the most crucial question in our journey to understand Dream Teams. Teams are made up of individual people, and in order to maximize our chances of those people coming together and making progress in The Zone, we need them to be willing to consider and adapt because of each other's diverse perspectives and heuristics. We need this kind of flexibility if we're going to make breakthrough progress together. No matter how well we get along, if we aren't willing to change our minds when necessary, we may as well work alone.

But what does it take for humans to become open-minded like that?

Philosophy professor Jason Baehr of Loyola Marymount University defines open-mindedness as follows:

"An open-minded person is characteristically (a) willing and (within limits) able (b) to transcend a default cognitive standpoint (c) in order to take up or take seriously the merits of (d) a distinct cognitive standpoint."

Dr. William Hare, one of the pioneers of research into open-mindedness, puts it another way. "It means being critically receptive to alternative possibilities," he says. "Being willing to think again despite having formed an opinion, and sincerely trying to avoid those conditions and offset those factors which constrain and distort our reflections."

Open-mindedness is not something a scientist can see by scanning your head. And, as I discovered when I conducted another one of my surveys (which we'll get to in more detail later), we're bad judges of how open-minded we actually are. Ninety-eight out of one hundred people claim to be more open-minded than average. By definition, of course, that can't be true.

For decades, the best thing psychologists had for measuring open-mindedness was a personality test called the Big Five. It asks people a series of questions like "To what extent do you agree with the following statement about yourself: I am always prepared." Or "I am curious about many different things." Based on how strongly you agree or disagree with the questions, you get a score for five categories. Agreeableness, Conscientiousness, Extraversion, Neuroticism, and Openness to Experience.

The trouble is that the test questions that determine openness to experience are things like "I have an active imagination," and "I have excellent ideas." Open-minded people generally say yes to these things, but so do other people. Openness to experience is about being willing to take in new information, not change our minds about it. Being willing to try a new flavor of ice cream is very different from becoming not racist or reversing course on a business strategy.

Typical personality tests for openness to experience, in other words, don't explain why Malcolm X changed course. Or why many people never change their minds about anything, from politics to religion to everyday opinions. X was open to debating his ideas with people who were very different from him, like Bayard Rustin. But debating over and over didn't change Malcolm's mind. Something else did.

Let's think about the magnitude of Malcolm's change of heart for a minute. He went from being a violent, racist fringe preacher to denouncing all three of those things. These—racial supremacy, violent separatism, and belief in the fringe leader Messenger Elijah—were part of his identity. They're what helped him get through prison and cope with the atrocities that white racists had done to him and his family. They saved his life.

This isn't a story about trying a new flavor of ice cream. He denounced his defining life philosophy. He went from the violent conservatism of racial separatism to integrationist and peacemaker. He went from disparaging the civil rights movement to becoming an invaluable part of the team.

If the Big Five's openness to experience isn't a good measure of that kind of open-mindedness, then what is?

The answer is something psychologists call "intellectual humility." As they put it, IH is a "nonthreatening awareness of one's intellectual fallibility." It's being willing to change our viewpoint without freaking out—and as of very recently, we can measure it.

As Drs. Elizabeth Krumrei-Mancuso and Stephen Rouse of Pepperdine University put it, "An intellectually humble person is able to find the right balance between dogmatically rejecting the dissenting viewpoints of others and yielding too quickly in the face of intellectual conflict." In 2016, Krumrei-Mancuso and Rouse published an assessment for IH that proved to be a breakthrough.

It turns out that ranking high on their IH test is associated with a whole bunch of open-minded things: openness to revising one's important opinions, curiosity, tolerance for ambiguity, low dogmatism, lower judgment of others based on their religious beliefs, less likelihood to demonize others for changing their attitudes, and being better able to detect the validity of persuasive arguments.*

Basically, it's the ability to keep one's own brain in The Zone.

This is exciting stuff. Tolerance for ambiguity. Lower judgment of others. Intellectual Humility isn't just the ability to change. It makes one more likely to correctly judge when it is time to change.

So now that we have an idea of how to measure open-mindedness, the big question is how do we get more of it?

---

*You can take said IH test online at shanesnow.com/dreamteams/ih.

3.

In the Bible, a militant religious enforcer named Saul went about persecuting and locking up followers of Jesus. Until one day, that is, when he had a miraculous change of heart. While he was traveling on the road to Damascus, the Angel of the Lord appeared to him.

After that vision, Saul the Christian persecutor became Paul the Christian apostle. He spent the rest of his life promoting the faith he once ridiculed. Half of the New Testament stems from Paul and the people he influenced.

The day Malcolm X's heart began to change, he didn't see an angel. He saw the hosts of heaven.

In 1964, X was in the middle of a crisis. He'd learned that prophet Elijah had been keeping a cadre of mistresses and fathered at least six children out of wedlock. He'd been abusing his power, taxing the members for his own gain. X wondered if Elijah wasn't a prophet after all.

He was put on probation for, among other things, discussing this with other ministers. While suspended, X decided to do something he had aspired to do for a long time—make a pilgrimage to the holy city of Mecca.

The pilgrimage involves journeying through the desert of Saudi Arabia and reenacting rituals established by the prophet Muhammad, in remembrance of Abraham and his family. It culminates in gigantic gatherings of Muslims from around the world praying together in harmony.

X was moved by the experience. "Islam brings together in unity all colors and classes," he wrote in his diary. "Everyone shares what he has, those who have share with those who have not, those who know teach those who don't know."

He saw pilgrims of every skin color treat each other with kindness. He saw people who in America would be classified as white who "were more genuinely brotherly than anyone else had ever been." And he saw brown and black people smiling and praying with them. It was like they even liked each other!*

And when he saw this, his heart started to soften.

Study after study shows that we have a hard time scrubbing our beliefs in things, even in the face of information that refutes them. This is how we preserve our self-identities.

Yet something interesting happens when we travel away from our identity-protecting home turf.

Research by Dr. Adam Galinsky of Columbia University and several of his colleagues finds that people who travel become better at "idea flexibility" or being able to solve problems in multiple ways.† Travel, their studies show, also "helps overcome functional fixedness."

In other words, being away from our safe home turf makes our minds more receptive to rethinking our old ideas.

Why is this? What's happening in our brains when we're in travel environments?

The first thing that occurs is the same thing that makes it easier for people to swear in a foreign language than their own. Research from the University of Warsaw finds that our "home" language is more emotionally connected to our identities, but when we speak in foreign languages, we become psychologically disembodied. When

---

* Given Malcolm X's public status at the time, he got a bit of VIP treatment on this trip that many others don't get. Yet still, the hajj process is a unifier overall, given that everyone is required to do the same things and share the same space together.

† Idea flexibility, often referred to as "lateral thinking," is the subject of my 2014 book, *Smartcuts*. Check shanesnow.com/smartcuts if you're interested!

we're in unfamiliar places, the lens through which we see the world becomes less connected to our precious identities.

This opens the door for something else to happen.

There's a concept in psychology called "balance theory" that explains why we like or dislike people and things by association, and how travel can help us change our minds about things that are connected to our identities.

Balance theory says that our brains don't like inconsistency. So when something is out of balance, our brains adjust to put it back.

It's like this:

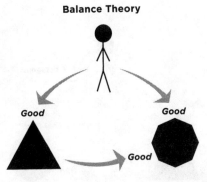

Say you have two beliefs. You think Triangles are good. You think that Octagons are good. You find out that Triangles are big fans of Octagons. This is great news for you, because you like them both. You are in balance.

However, if you find out that Triangles think Octagons are bad, you become out of balance. You can't think highly of both Triangles and Octagons if Triangles think Octagons are bad.

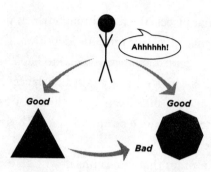

This will bother your brain until one of two things happens. Either you'll decide that Octagons must be bad:

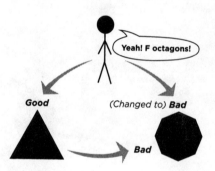

Or you'll decide that you're wrong about Triangles:

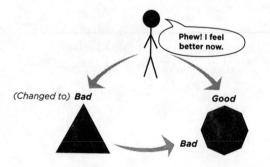

When we embed ourselves in places with a different culture from our own, we often get confronted with paradoxes about our beliefs. We realize that the way we have balanced the world may not actually line up. We're faced with the choice of either rebalancing the equation, or decoupling the things we've associated—which can be extraordinarily difficult.

Laboratory research shows that many of the things we are biased about—the negative associations we have with things—are the result of our brains trying to balance things out with our prior beliefs, not the result of rational arguments.

For example, when psychologists put people in rooms and have them list arguments on both sides of a tricky issue—say, abortion or animal testing—people tend to list more arguments in favor of whichever side they believe in. But then when researchers prompt them, most people are able to come up with additional arguments for the opposing side without difficulty. "It seems that individuals have these counter-arguments stored in memory but they don't draw on them when first asked," write researchers from the University of Pennsylvania.

When we travel outside of our home environment, our brains can start to let go of the barriers that prevent us from properly analyzing the information for or against our prior beliefs.

This can lead to a couple of results. Since we're less tethered to our ego, travel experiences can make it easy for us to change our minds about things:

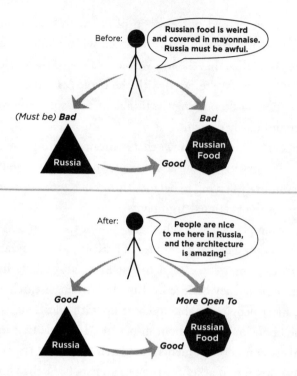

Visiting unfamiliar places primes us to decouple things our brains automatically link via balance theory. Traveling helps us to decategorize people and cultures and pick apart stereotypes from individuals, like the Eagles and the Rattlers did with each other did during scout camp.

This was the big epiphany that Malcolm X had when he went to Mecca.

"I have eaten from the same plate, drank from the same glass, slept on the same bed or rug, while praying to the same God . . . with fellow Muslims whose skins was the whitest of white, whose eyes were the bluest of blue . . . [for] the first time in my life . . . I didn't see them as 'white' men," he wrote. It "forced me to 'rearrange' much of my own thought-pattern and to toss aside some of my previous conclusions."

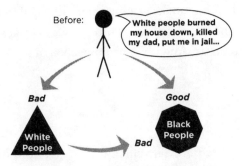

It was impossible to hold on to the idea that white people were all bad after hanging out with and feeling connected to so many good ones. The only choice X had was to either decide that Muslims were bad, or that he was wrong in his generalization about white people. In other words, he had to break apart the elements of his balance theory loop.

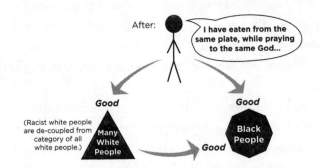

X's daughter would later say, "The more he traveled, the freer he became. The freer we all became."

This is where the prevailing narrative on Malcolm X's transformation generally stops. He traveled and, like Saul, he saw the light. However, the 2011 Pulitzer-winning biography by the wonderful Marable Manning* makes an important distinction that most people miss—and data confirm. Travel alone isn't always enough to change our minds. And it wasn't quite enough for Malcolm, either.

A half century after Malcolm X came back from Mecca, a young white man from southern Florida made a similar journey, in reverse.

Derek Black was the godson of David Duke, the head of the Ku Klux Klan, and the son of Don Black, the founder of Stormfront, the world's then-largest white nationalist website. At an early age, Derek got heavily involved in the white nationalist movement, writing essays, calling into radio shows, and working to convert other young people to the cause of separating the races. By age nineteen he'd won a county election on a thinly veiled white nationalist platform and embarked on a quest to get other white nationalists in office to combat racial integration around the United States. He was seen by the Klan and other groups as something of a "chosen one" among separatists, anti-Semites, and white supremacists.

And then he moved across the state for college. He started hanging out with kids from all sorts of backgrounds, with all sorts of beliefs. He made friends with an observant Jewish student who invited him to Shabbat dinners. "He just wanted to let me see a Jewish

---

* And sadly, now deceased.

community thing so that if I was going to keep saying these anti-Semitic things that at least I had seen real Jews," Black later told the *New York Times*.

And then he changed his mind.

Living among these other kinds of people opened his heart. He allowed himself to consider information he wouldn't have before, such as evidence disproving the erroneous "science" he relied on about race and IQ.

"I have these two experiences, and I have a lot of trouble reconciling them sometimes," he said. But balance theory sorted him out, and Black soon became a spokesperson against the thing he once campaigned for.

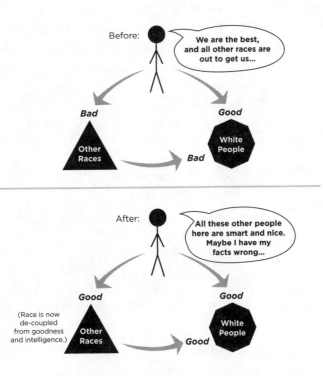

Stories like these are encouraging. But certainly there are plenty of people who travel to Mecca or move to college who don't change their entire lives around. What's really going on when a Malcolm X or a Derek Black changes his mind?

In 2016, armed with Dr. Krumrei-Mancuso's and Dr. Rouse's research, I put together an IH assessment with some additional questions of mine to dig into this question.* I ran a study of thousands of people around the United States to look at the ways that people with different amounts of open-mindedness live their lives.

Predictably, my study found a strong correlation between being well traveled and having intellectual humility. However, it unearthed an even stronger correlation that helps us understand what makes the difference between those who travel and change their minds, and those who travel and don't.

It turns out that people who actually *live* in foreign places are even more likely to have high IH than those who just visit. Living in a foreign country for three to six months has a stronger effect on IH than visiting ten countries.

---

*Which you can take at shanesnow.com/dreamteams/om.

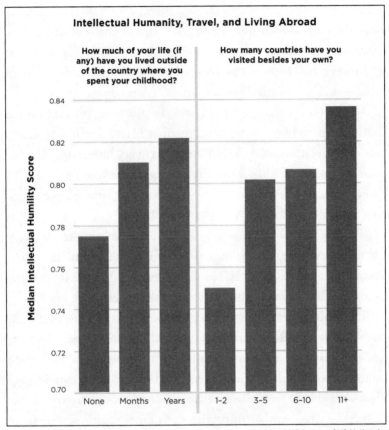

Source: shanesnow.com 2017 Survey of US Nationals

This confirms for intellectual humility what other studies had deduced about openness to experience: just visiting other countries and observing their cultures as tourists is not nearly as good at building openness as becoming embedded in those cultures. (Unless, as we can see from the data, you visit a *lot* of countries, which in turn would mean you've probably spent a significant amount of time outside of your own culture.) You can visit a new or strange place without trying the food or opening up to the idea that the way people live and speak and think in this new place is valid. But it's hard to *live* somewhere and not become a little more open to the culture.

Dr. Galinsky and his colleagues found that graduate students who had lived abroad were more likely to consider out-of-the-box solutions to problems in group projects than people who didn't, or who just visited. Fashion designers who lived abroad produced more creative and successful designs than those who didn't.

We might on the one hand conclude that open-minded people would be more likely to travel in the first place, which is probably true. However, my study found something very interesting that indicates a more causal relationship. Not everyone who had high IH had traveled, but almost everyone who had lived in multiple countries ranked high for IH.

The key insight about becoming open-minded through travel is not mere exposure. It's the idea of becoming "multicultural." Being able to hold multiple cultural ideas in one's head at the same time. Being able to live with multiple balance theory charts at once.

Dr. Galinsky and his colleagues found that "biculturals," or people who identified with two cultures, "exhibited more fluency, flexibility, and novelty on a creative uses task and produced more innovations at work than did assimilated or separated individuals." They were able to demonstrate that people who came from multiple cultures or who could identify with two or more cultures were more able to use lateral thinking—the application of open-mindedness—at work.*

And it turns out that when an individual's head is diverse in terms of languages spoken, that individual becomes physically more open-minded.

---

*The Economist Intelligence Unit shows that two-thirds of business teams that are multicultural are more innovative. The European Union's DYLAN Project found that mixed-language work teams have a greater propensity to solve problems, which is something we'd expect to hear at this point after all our time studying Problem Mountain.

I don't mean that one's head literally opens up. But neuroscientists find that multilingual people's brains do look physically different. Learning to speak multiple languages helps us to realize that there is not just one right way to say something, and that the way of saying something that we grew up saying can be less precise than someone else's way. This leads our brains to wire up a little more linguistic humility. As linguist Gabrielle Hogan-Brun explains, "The left inferior parietal cortex—an area of the brain heavily involved in the processing of language, forming concepts, and thinking abstractly—is denser in bilinguals than monolinguals, and becomes denser as language proficiency increases."

This change in brain makeup leads to more emotional understanding of other people, less fear of loss—meaning more progress in the war between reason and the amygdalae—and more rationality when it comes to changing one's mind. The more we adjust our balance theory charts, the more our brains change, and the easier it gets to adjust in the future.

In other words, the key to intellectual humility is increasing the cognitive diversity inside our own heads.

When Malcolm X made his pilgrimage to Mecca, he had already taken a bit of a hit to his ego. He'd been edged out of the spotlight at his own mosque, and he'd warmed up a bit to the idea that Elijah might not have all the answers he said he did.

As we saw from his first conversion from drug dealer to preacher, X had the ability in him to change his mind. But his views had calcified over the years. His heart had hardened toward a whole lot of people.

The trip to Mecca started softening it. But when you look at his letters and interviews and sermons in 1964 and 1965, it's clear that X's subsequent five months *living* in Africa were what truly opened his mind.

After Mecca, he spent some time in the United States formulating new ideas, and then he went to Ghana, Egypt, and other countries in Africa to develop a more multicultural perspective. It was there that X fully embraced what would become his new rallying cry. The struggle for equality wasn't just about civil rights, he realized. It was about human rights.

"His Middle East and Africa experiences had greatly broadened his mind," wrote Marable in his Malcolm X biography. "It was the romance with Africa itself, its beauty, diversity, and complexity" that helped Malcolm transform.

X's philosophy on race, X wrote, changed after living among "thousands of people of different races and colors who treated me as a human being."

4.

Malcolm Little was thirty-nine years old the second time racists burned his house down. This time, however, he wasn't surprised. He'd known the dangers inherent to changing his mind and breaking with the Nation of Islam. He did it anyway.

Before he split from the NOI, X had already become an amazing case study in coalition building. He'd used powerful shared hatred of a common enemy to attract listeners to his speeches. He then used those speeches as a platform to get his ideas on the superordinate values of the Nation of Islam to a mass audience.

Unfortunately, when his values changed, his former allies turned on him.

After the house burned down, X moved to a hotel. He continued building the mosque he'd started after his conversion to Sunni Islam, and he went to work on his nonreligious organization to advance human rights. It was during one of his public speeches for this that a gang of Nation of Islam members—possibly with ties to law enforcement who knew of X's change of heart but were still afraid of him anyway—shot him to death in front of his family and friends.

Malcolm X's autobiography would go on to sell millions of copies—despite the fact that a small percentage of his life was spent living along the lines of Islamic orthodoxy. (In fact, people flocked to his book in large part because of his transformation story.) And X's teachings would influence tens of millions, helping generations better understand racism, human rights, Afro-American culture, and the perspective of a people who'd been beaten down and abused for centuries.

Despite his untimely death, X made a sizable contribution to the Dream Team that pushed civil rights forward. The movement needed X's cognitive diversity, his perspective on the poor northern black man, his self-empowerment and pride, and his heuristics for motivating and mobilizing. Combined with the perspectives and heuristics of the pacifistic Bayard Rustin, the eloquent King, and many others, the movement made historic progress.

As we see from the history that ensued, civil rights needed more than a group of angry separatists to succeed. It needed moderates and liberals and conservatives to mobilize together. It needed them to link arms with people of all races to fight together as a team. It needed what Malcolm X realized in his most powerful epiphany from living in Africa:

"Separation is not the goal of the Afro-American," he told a packed crowd of 1,500 people at Chicago's Civic Opera House shortly before his assassination. "Nor is integration his goal. They are merely methods toward his real end—respect as a human being."

The superordinate group of mankind could only come together with that respect. "The true believer," X wrote in his diary while traveling, "recognizes the oneness of humanity."

In order for him to get to that point, X needed to put himself in an environment where his mind could become open to the truth—that the world was not as black-and-white as the KKK or NOI or balance theory would have him think.

Dr. King said X's murder was a "great tragedy" and that it had deprived "the world of a potentially great leader."

This is striking, because King and X had been philosophical opponents for years. X was becoming more nonviolent and King-like in his last months, but he was still more hardened than King ever was.

In all those years, King had respected X even though he disagreed. But over time, King began adapting some of his own ideas because of X. In his later speeches, King started preaching about black self-pride, an important message of X's that the civil rights movement had hardly emphasized at that point. Shortly before King was assassinated, the journalist David Halberstam reported that King "sounded like a nonviolent Malcolm X."

While King was a political revolutionary, X was a cultural revolutionary, says author James Cone. That cultural revolution eventually became part of King's political philosophy. "Malcolm changed how black people thought about themselves. Before Malcolm came along, we were all Negroes. After Malcolm, he helped us become black."

X's change of heart allowed him to help push civil rights leaders a little further than they might have on their own. And X's personal journey of open-mindedness made him a catalyst the movement needed.

It's clear from the mountains of books and essays written on X and King that they each had a high amount of intellectual humility.

They were both willing to change, accept, and hold steady when occasion needed. King was able to use that—and Malcolm X's contributions—to build the Dream Team coalition of people and ideas that got the Civil Rights Act passed.

I'll confess that I'm a cliché when it comes to Malcolm X. Growing up, I initially liked him because of the part where he stopped calling white people devils. But as I dug into his story, something else happened to me that helped me open to other parts of his message and made me love the man beyond what was in my personal interest because of my identity.

I would have my own change of heart about Malcolm X, and perhaps more important, about the art of respect and working together because of him. Buried in my IH data was the surprising reason why—and a key to developing open-mindedness in ourselves and in others that doesn't require the privilege or funds to travel across the world.

八

OXYTOCIN, A LOVE STORY

"I'll admit it—I hated him!"

1.

Fumiko Nakamura and her husband, Takekuma, would have never guessed, at the time they were thrust out of their Los Angeles home at gunpoint, that their son George would someday be a massive celebrity.

The odds of this would have seemed remote even if the young family and all of their Japanese neighbors weren't being rounded up like cattle, forced to live in stables, then prison camps. Truth was that 1942 wasn't just the height of Japanophobia in California. It was the high-water mark of anti-Asian prejudice in America generally.

The law at the time said that Asian-born people were not allowed to become US citizens because of their race's alleged inability to assimilate. Asian children born in America were natural citizens by default, but they rarely attained white-collar jobs or even worked outside their own communities. A few decades before, California had been the site of the biggest mass-lynching in US history. The victims were Chinese immigrants. Since the mid-1800s, the Chinese and the Japanese had occupied the bottom rungs of California's social ladder, alongside Koreans, Filipinos, Vietnamese, and East Indians.

Stereotypes were abundant. The year 1913 saw the debut of the fictional arch-villain "Fu Manchu," brainchild of British novelist Sax Rohmer. Scheming, soulless, crafty-yet-primitive, Fu Manchu embodied every Western suspicion toward the inscrutable East.*

And there was Charlie Chan: a fictional Chinese American detective who delivered ornate sentences in garbled syntax. Pudgy and nonthreatening, Chan is frequently and profusely apologetic for the fact that he happens to be Chinese. Part hero and part stooge, Charlie Chan represented the white ideal of the deferential minority every Asian American ought to be.

Then on December 7, 1941, the empire of Japan attacked the US fleet at Pearl Harbor and awakened the sleeping giant that was America's war machine. A flood of anti-Japanese propaganda followed. Japanese men were simian, "yellow," subhuman. Japanese women were either concubines, geishas, or maids—the unthinking attachées of their male overlords.

On the heels of Pearl Harbor, President Roosevelt made the mistake of a lifetime. He signed Executive Order 9066, permitting the military to lock up of over 120,000 people of Japanese ancestry without trial or due process of law.

Most of those imprisoned were natural-born US citizens. Half were children. The reason given—unconstitutional on its face—was that Japanese Americans might "sympathize" with America's new enemy. But a congressional commission would later admit that the order was "motivated largely by racial prejudice." White business owners were happy to see Japanese American competitors rounded up and incarcerated, and California's powerful agriculture lobby was

---

*Rohmer's Sherlock to this Asian Moriarty is the hero detective Denis Nayland-Smith—*Sir* Denis Nayland-Smith, no less. Nayland-Smith is chiseled, brave, resourceful, and, of course, English.

particularly eager to uproot Japanese American farmers and replace them with whites.*

Fumiko was a US citizen, born near Sacramento. Takekuma was born in Japan, but he'd immigrated to San Francisco at age sixteen. The United States wouldn't allow him to become a citizen even though he'd lived in the country more than two decades and was working hard to provide for his family. Now forty, Takekuma, who went by "Norman," had saved money to buy a home. But Norman's American dream was torn away when the US military stormed his neighborhood. He and Fumiko, aka "Emily," and their three small children were "relocated" to the Rohwer War Relocation Center: a prison camp situated in a virtual swamp in rural southeast Arkansas.†

George was five years old when Norman told the kids they were "going on a vacation." He was old enough to realize that this vacation was not a choice. Inside the camp he would play with friends outdoors while guards in surveillance towers trained machine guns on them. At the camp school the children recited the Pledge of Allegiance. Little George could see barbed wire through the window. *With liberty and justice for all.*

Three years later the family was released. Their home was gone. "It was a devastating blow to my parents," George later recalled. The only job Norman could get was washing dishes in Chinatown.

Back at school in LA, young George was ambitious. He wanted to be an architect. Maybe even an actor! One day he might even go into politics. Become a public speaker. Get married . . .

---

*After all, America was fighting Germany and Italy, too. But, needless to say, neither Henry Schwartz, senator of Wyoming, nor Louis Capozzoli, representative of New York, ever saw his family summarily locked up for the duration of the war.

†The family was later transferred to the Tule Lake War Relocation Center in California, where they were confined until President Roosevelt suspended Japanese internment in December 1944.

He was too young to know how long the odds were. In postwar America, the average Asian American worker made less than the average African American—which was itself a third lower than the average white. Young George had an uphill battle ahead.

- Asian American Fortune 500 CEOs? Zero.
- Asian American movie stars? Zero.
- Asian American senators and congresspeople? You guessed it. Zero.

Race wasn't the only obstacle George faced. He had something else going against him when it came to fulfilling his dreams.

Something he hadn't told anyone.

2.

Let's pause here for just a moment. I want you to read something. The following quotations are from five different world-class athletes. I want you to read them, and then I'll have a few questions for you:

> *"No one can ever brainwash me to make me believe that Sugar Ray Robinson and Muhammad Ali was better than me."*

> *"Bask in my glory . . . I am the greatest athlete to live."*

> *"I run New York. I run this whole city."*

> *"I see me being a designer. I see me being a model. I see me being a TV star."*

"If you want to win, sometimes you have to have a difficult conversation with people. . . . You know they are not going to like you, but you do it because you want what is best for the team."

From these quotes alone, which of these athletes would you rather have as a teammate? As a boss?

Which do you think is the better team player?

Even athletes who compete alone are part of a team. The best boxers and swimmers and sprinters in the world have coaches and helpers and trainers and nutritionists and managers who help them break records. But as you may have guessed, the last quote is the only person on the list who actually plays a team sport, and coincidentally the only one of these five pros who is particularly humble. Her name is Carla Overbeck, and she's the former captain of the world-champion US women's soccer team that dominated the sport in the 1990s. The others, in order, are Floyd Mayweather Jr., Usain Bolt, Conor McGregor, and Ryan Lochte. Each is famous for his arrogance and attitude.

Floyd Mayweather? Incredible boxer. And he's right! He's probably better than Ali. He's probably better than Sugar Ray Robinson.

But he's not a better *collaborator*. Floyd Mayweather may have a team, but he doesn't play well with others.*

Overbeck, on the other hand, wasn't just a star athlete. She's also a star mom, co-coach of college soccer teams, and an inspiration to her players. When she was playing soccer herself, she was notorious for personally carrying their luggage on the road, for being the last team member to hit the showers. Mayweather and the boys may be

---

*When he was the world's highest-paid athlete, Mayweather—owner of three Bugattis and three US Golden Gloves awards—punched his girlfriend in front of their little sons, warning the boys to not leave the house or call 911, or "I'll beat you." Fair fight? The world-champion welterweight versus the elementary schoolers?

great athletes, but you wouldn't really want to work on a group project with them.

In his book *The Captain Class*, Sam Walker, the *Wall Street Journal* sports editor whom we mentioned earlier,* discovered that every one of the world's greatest sports dynasties had something surprising in common: their players, and in particular their team captains, had a whole lot of humility.[†]

For example, the Boston Celtics basketball team that dominated the NBA in the late 1950s through the 1960s, "never had any individual member whose isolated performance ranked among the best in history. In seven of its eleven championship seasons, it didn't place a single scorer in the top ten" of the league—yet it destroyed its opponents. Team captain Bill Russell in particular, Walker points out, was a crucial collaborator, and he led his team to so much victory precisely because he didn't seek his own glory. Overbeck, when captain of the US women's national soccer team during its famous winning streak in the 1990s, posted only seven goals in her international career, yet she led her team to dominate the world. This pattern of humility holds in rugby, volleyball, cricket, you name it.

We see this in the way that our Soviet hockey players interacted with each other, compared to their North American counterparts. The Russians described their job on the ice as that of being "servants" to the puck. And the player who held the puck was not out for his own glory, but to serve the other players. Nobody was trying to maximize his statistics, nobody cared who scored the goal. Nobody was sad when the plan had to change and the crowd cheered for someone else's smart move.

---

*Again, I am not a sports guy, and this one was fascinating anyway!

[†]Among other things, including a willingness to think about the rules and game play differently than others did. Sounds like they have a fair amount of Mark Tigan or Nellie Bly to them.

A team is more likely to become elite, Walker's research shows, "if it has a captain that leads from the shadows." And crucially, every Dream Team in sports, as Walker defines it, "had open, talkative cultures in which grievances were aired, strategies discussed, and criticisms leveled without delay."* Humility allows these teams to have hard conversations without blowing up. *You do it because you want what is best for the team.*

Does this remind you of our friend Robert Diggs, captain of the Wu-Tang Clan? The RZA's primary role was to make beats and create an environment where his team members could battle productively and thrive. Wu-Tang was unafraid to spar, and when necessary, RZA put family before ego.

Jean Laffite and General Jackson? Same idea, for a brief time. ULT and WebCT? Bly and the New York government? Same pattern. Malcolm X and Martin Luther King Jr. demonstrate it, too. In each case, the team members sacrificed their pride and self-interest to the overarching goal of climbing higher together.

This isn't just humility; it's intellectual humility. It requires being open to and willing to change when change is hard.

Our complexity as individuals is what gives us the chance to do amazing things together. But we have to be willing to change our hearts and minds or it won't work. The more IH a group's individuals have between them, the better the chances they have of harnessing their tension, because they are able to actually adapt in light of new perspectives and heuristics and information.

IH, in other words, is the thing that puts us at the top of The Zone:

---

*The original US men's Olympic basketball "Dream Team" in 1992 reportedly had a rough time in practice initially, as too many alpha players butted heads. But things clicked into place when Magic Johnson relinquished the need to be top dog and decided to let Michael Jordan be the star. The tension between the two of them led to a compromise that, while not necessarily humble on both sides, helped the team get out of its own way.

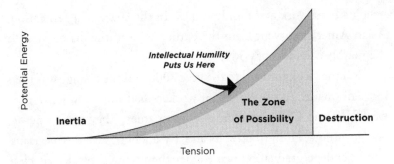

In this final chapter, we're going to dig into one of the most powerful tools for making the human brain become more intellectually humble. We're going to unlock the kind of open-mindedness we need to become dream *collaborators*.

3.

A strange thing happened in the thirty years that elapsed between the start of World War II and the end of the Vietnam conflict: the wage gap between white men and Asian American men disappeared. At the time of the Japanese internment, Asian American men made 30 percent less on average than their white counterparts. But by the time Saigon fell to North Vietnamese forces in 1975, Asian men in America were earning only about 5 percent less than white men.

Asian Americans had become a fantastic case study in the American Dream. Their collective economic outlook had gone from dishwasher-slash-suspected-saboteur to white-collar professional. Now there were Asian American doctors, lawyers, professors, businesspeople. Newspapers that once said "Orientals" had "most of the vices and few of the virtues of the African," now applauded Asian people's hard work and family values. In the space of a generation, Asian Americans went from the barbed wire of the prison yard to the marble corridors of power.

Roll the clock forward to the year 2000 and the change was even more dramatic: Asian American workers had high-end jobs. They were VPs and CEOs of blue-chip companies. They were senators and governors, Hollywood stars and TV anchors. Asian Americans' rate of college graduation was higher than whites, blacks, or Hispanics.

The image of the upwardly mobile Asian American became a stereotype in itself. While social scientists warned that racism and discrimination persisted, political pundits were already weaponizing the Asian miracle, lecturing other groups on what they needed to do to become the next "model minority."

The incredible turnaround for Asian Americans was good news for people like our young friend George. There was just one tiny problem with the political talking points, though.

They get what happened totally wrong.

Narrowing the earnings gap from 30 percent to 5 percent is a big improvement, especially when African American stats hardly budged. So what happened? If the mainstream perception of Asian Americans went from "degenerate" in the 1940s to "role model" in the 1980s, what changed? Had Japanese, Chinese, Vietnamese, Taiwanese, Korean, Filipino, Mongolian, and Malaysian Americans suddenly abandoned their own traditions and culture in favor of white American culture? Had they developed a new work ethic?

No. Research from economists like Brown University's Dr. Nathaniel Hilger shows that the real reason Asians started to do better in America was not because they suddenly got better family values, and not because they suddenly started working harder. Asians didn't go from "lazy" to "responsible."

It was simply because America became less racist toward them.

In a generation, the same hardworking Asian American doing the same job got paid more fairly. In two generations, he was getting paid even better. Meanwhile, the same Asian American student earning the same grades had better odds of getting into a leading university. Asians became outsize beneficiaries of affirmative action,* and a positively reinforcing cycle was created as even more Asians graduated from college and obtained top jobs. The United States was becoming more attractive to Asian-born professionals—enough to outweigh the risk and hardship of immigrating to America. So more Asians with advanced degrees came over. The children of Asian immigrants could grow up in a country where their opportunities were nearly equal to whites'. Unlike young Malcolm Little, a counselor could realistically encourage an Asian American high school kid to "hitch your wagon to a star."†

"Asian Americans—some of them at least—have made tremendous progress in the United States," writes economics journalist Jeff Guo. "But the greatest thing that ever happened to them wasn't that they studied hard, or that they benefited from tiger moms or Confucian values. It's that other Americans started treating them with a little more respect."

But why? Why just them?

The answer is the last piece in our puzzle.

---

*For the first decades of it, at least.

† Ralph Waldo Emerson, *Society and Solitude*, 1870.

4.

Two generations after America started changing its mind about Asian people, a similar sea change happened for another persecuted group: gay people.

Homosexuality has existed in every culture and every corner of the globe as far back as history goes. References to romantic love between two men or two women show up as early as the Egyptian pharaohs of the third millennium BCE, Hammurabi in ancient Babylon, and the Zhou dynasty of classical China. Homosexuality was celebrated in Assyria, tolerated in Persia, and embraced in Ancient Greece.

Then, in the first century BCE, homosexuality was criminalized in Roman Britain, as it was throughout the Roman world. Fifteen centuries later homosexual behavior was declared punishable by death during the reign of Henry VIII.* And by the 1800s, homosexuality was illegal almost everywhere.

As such, feelings of same-sex attraction were kept secret by the millions of Western men and women who felt them.†

When our young friend George reentered public school after his family's forced internment, he started to notice there was something

---

*(Though that didn't stop kings from taking male lovers.)

† The Oscar Wilde trials were possibly the first instance of mass interest in the disclosure of said secret. After a series of public hearings, Wilde was convicted of the "indecency" of being gay, though not for any particular action, and sent to prison camp. The irony of this should not be lost on us.

different about him. He was baffled when his friends started getting excited about girls. "How could girls be so interesting to them?" he wondered.

Now, boys, on the other hand . . .

While his friends ogled the cover girls on fashion magazines, George was drawn to the muscle mags in the corner, where chiseled beefcakes* flexed. Teenage George knew these feelings would not win him points. At the time, half of America believed that gay people shouldn't be allowed to hold jobs. More than half believed homosexual activity merited jail time.

And as for high school, well, kids can be cruel.

Think, for a moment, about what being a gay, Japanese teenager in America in the 1950s must have felt like. People didn't trust you or think you were smart because of the way you looked. People would want to put you in jail if they found out who you loved. Your friends talked to you like you were straight. The only thing that could be worse would be if they found out you weren't.

So George kept his feelings to himself.

But here's what's fascinating. Except for a short-lived dip during the AIDS epidemic, public support for gay rights climbed during every decade after the 1960s, with a significant uptick in the 2000s. Here's what it looked like:

---

*Resembling your author, no doubt.

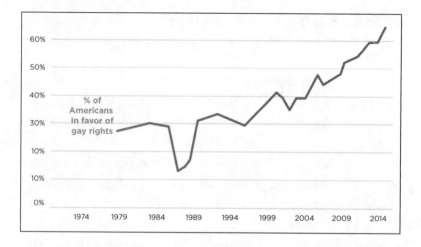

This wasn't just coastal liberals. This was everyone. People became more accepting in religions that deem homosexuality offensive to God. Pew Research showed a growing percentage in favor of equal LGBT rights among every major American religious group.

Within a generation, the majority of Americans were saying it was okay for someone who felt differently from them to love who they wanted to love. At the very least, the sentiment became, those differences shouldn't be cause for loss of rights.

What could explain this phenomenon? We learned in the previous chapter about how traveling to—and living among—foreign cultures helps to open our minds. But the millions of Americans who changed their minds about Asian immigrants between 1945 and 2000 didn't all spend a gap year in Asia. And there wasn't some magical Gaytopia across the sea to convince straight Americans that gay people weren't so scary after all.*

These two changes in attitude happened at somewhat different

---

*Although I would totally visit that place!

times. Other groups like African Americans, Arabs, and Latinos would have much less luck.

And yet, one of the main factors driving these two shifts in the American psyche would ultimately be the same.

5.

For several years, George's dream of being a famous actor was remote as ever. After getting his architecture degree, he went to theater school and began auditioning. Most parts available to a Japanese man in Hollywood in the late 1950s and early 1960s were fairly cheesy. Hysterical nitwit side characters. Skeevy Fu Manchu types. When his rich bass voice got him a gig doing English voice-over for the American release of *Godzilla Raids Again*, George was ecstatic. But he was still swimming against the tide.

George didn't tell people he was gay. His square jaw and deep voice lent themselves to the heterosexual ideal of Hollywood in its Golden Age, so he played into it.

At the time, television portrayed homosexuals as either violent criminals or mentally ill. In one early TV episode—*Marcus Welby, M.D.*—a man comes to the doctor suffering depression and diabetes. Dr. Welby diagnoses him with "homosexuality," but assures him that one day he could become "normal." Other episodes painted gay people as pedophiles and rapists. The first group of lesbians on TV that I could find were homicidal killers in the show *Police Woman*. These tropes ignored, of course, the fact that murder and rape exist at no higher rates among gays than among straights.

Over time, however, television's gay stories started to get more realistic. In the 1972 made-for-TV movie *That Certain Summer*,

Martin Sheen and Hal Holbrook played gentlemen who lived together in secret. Another early gay character was Billy Crystal in *Soap*.* Crystal was lovable and captivating, though his character was made to flirt with the idea of getting a sex change, as if this were something that gay people would all want.

Progress was slow, and offensive stereotypes persisted. But, over time, gay characters got more sympathetic, and they got more airtime. When fan-favorite Ellen DeGeneres came out on TV in 1997—both as herself and as her fictional character Ellen Morgan—forty-two million people tuned in. The tide had turned. Gay was mainstream. Major networks started airing more shows with recurring gay characters.

Here's a graph of the number of recurring gay television characters from 1970 to 2015:

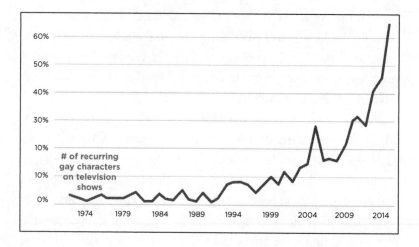

---

*French cinema had a sympathetic gay character—albeit one who never appeared on-screen—at least as early as the 1957 farce *Les Oeufs de l'autruche* ("The Ostrich Has Two Eggs"). 1964's *Les amitiés particulières*—adapted from the 1943 novel of the same title—featured a more authentic portrayal of boys in a French Catholic boarding school.

It shouldn't be too surprising that as the number of people with positive attitudes toward gay people increased, so, too, did the way we portrayed gay people on television. In fact, here's a representation of the increase of the word "gay" in movie and television scripts between 1965 and now, compared to the decline of a common gay slur in movie and TV scripts during the same time period, according to data from Ben Schmidt's and Erez Aidan's Bookworm Project:

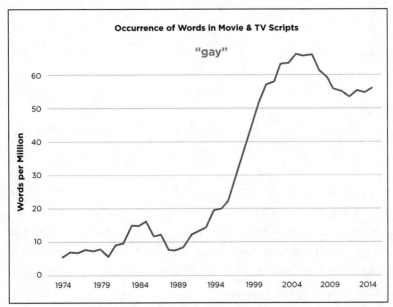

Data courtesy of Ben Schmidt and Culturomics.org

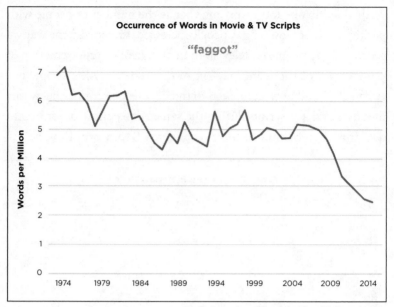

Data courtesy of Ben Schmidt and Culturomics.org

And there's something intriguing hidden in these charts. When we overlay them with our first chart of gay acceptance milestones and account for the lag time between when scripts are written and when they hit screens (which can take years), we can see that we have things backward. Hollywood didn't follow gay acceptance. Hollywood actually *predicted* it.

We might conclude from this that Hollywood is just slightly ahead of the curve when it comes to social issues.

But as is often the case, there was something even more interesting going on.

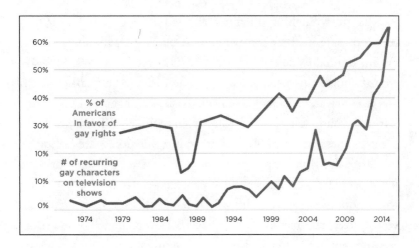

6.

A decade after Ellen came out, a group of people went to the theater for an unusual movie experience. The film was the latest James Bond movie—the British spy franchise created by Ian Fleming. But there was a catch! This wasn't going to be the usual Pepsi-and-popcorn diversion. This particular audience was going to watch the film while hooked up to an array of equipment that, from the look of it, might have come out of Q's own lab.

The man behind this science experiment was neuro-economist Paul Zak of Claremont University. While the audience watched Bond tangle with villains and flirt with disaster, Zak saw what he called "an amazing neural ballet." The James Bond story line, his instruments demonstrated, changed the activity in the audience's brains.

And that brain activity made their bodies do curious things. When Bond sidled along the edge of a building, bad guys closing in, the audience's heart rates increased. Palms began to sweat. When Bond was in a tight spot, their brains registered fear. When Bond faced a gut-wrenching dilemma, the audience tensed up as if they did, too. Safe in their comfy chairs, Bond's spectators were living out his drama inside their minds.

Of course this experience is common to virtually all of us.* If you've ever watched a movie or been to a baseball game or comforted a friend, you've felt it. So why do we empathize? Why do we—to a greater or lesser extent—feel what we imagine others are feeling?

Dr. Zak's Bond experiment showed something that surprised a lot of people. A certain neurochemical happens to be responsible for this emotional mirroring. It's a little molecule called oxytocin. Previously, oxytocin was known to play a role in pregnancy and breastfeeding, but not in much else. And certainly not in action movies.

What Zak discovered is that this molecule is key to how we become open to other people and their ideas.

"Oxytocin is produced when we are trusted or shown a kindness, and it motivates cooperation with others," Zak explains. "It does this by enhancing the sense of empathy, our ability to experience others' emotions." Empathy, of course, was important for our survival as humans. As Zak put it, "It allows us to understand how others are likely to react to a situation, including those with whom we work."

To prove this, Zak had people snort synthetic oxytocin and watch TV ads for charities. He allowed the test subjects to donate to any of the charities if they wanted. And guess what? The people who snorted oxytocin were 57 percent more likely to give to a charity they saw in one of the ads, and they donated 56 percent more than others. Overall, the oxytocin-huffers reported feeling more concern for the people in the advertisements.

Here's where it gets really interesting. Zak then conducted the

---

*Starting around roughly age two, though it can be earlier or later depending on the individual.

same charity ad experiments without making anyone snort any-thing. He wanted to see what kinds of natural interactions between people would lead to oxytocin production. What makes our brains make more of it in real life?

What he discovered is the neuroscientific basis for one of the most marvelous and useful techniques for building openness to other humans.

In hindsight, the epiphany was simple. In one experiment, Dr. Zak had people watch charity advertisements with a narrative story line versus ads without any story. Imagine, for example, a father talking about how his child was struggling with cancer, or an animal shelter employee describing how a pet was abused—versus ads with heart-breaking statistics about child cancer rates or pet abuse. Zak found that stories motivated people to donate significantly more money than ads that just delivered straight facts. When he analyzed test subjects' blood, Zak found that the people who'd seen the ads with stories had higher oxytocin levels. Stories stimulated oxytocin production in the brain.

In the James Bond experiment, in addition to the racing hearts and sweating palms, it turned out that Zak's equipment also showed that the audience's brains made more oxytocin. Through this and similar studies, Zak's lab discovered that anytime people experience character-driven stories, their brains pump out more oxytocin.

While not *specifically* searching for a love potion,* Dr. Zak had stumbled upon the chemical explanation for what centuries of poets already knew.

Stories help us fall in love. They build relationships and make us care.

This idea goes back to before we even had pens to write stories down. In preliterate societies, myths and stories were the embodi-

---

*He claims.

ment of our shared identity. They made it easier for us to work and to survive together. In a world without Google Calendar, stories helped us package and retain information. Our tribe's daily minutiae—and our tribe's ethos and lore—were alike passed by word of mouth, campfire to campfire, generation to generation. Relating and remembering stories was hardwired into our growing brains.*

While stories were a great way to package information, they also held clues for who and what we should care about. The caring part was oxytocin's job. If a story was about a character—someone whose cooperation might be important for our survival—our brain would generate the kind of activity that helped us remember that person and care about them. Oxytocin's role, in part, was to get our bodies to mimic what our tribesmates were doing—from breathing to sweating to body language to emotion. If someone was part of our tribe, our brains wanted us to be, run, jump, and remember along with them.

A big moment in gay television history was the 2009 debut of the fictional Kurt Hummel, played by Chris Colfer in the TV musical *Glee*.

Kurt wasn't a token. He was an ordinary, awkward teenager coming to terms with being different and growing up—something that every teen and former teen can relate to, gay or not. He's outspoken, sensitive, courageous, and charismatic. As the story unfolds, Kurt has to face bullies at school, come out to his father, and come

---

*And it turned out that because stories engage more of our senses, they help us remember that information better, too. Scientists have a saying that "neurons that fire together wire together." This means that when we learn something through a story that, say, evokes imagery and emotion, more neurons activate, and our brains retain the information better.

to terms with a host of confusing feelings. *Glee* gave millions of straight viewers a window into what it's actually like to grow up gay. And, as gay journalist Alexander Stevenson put it, "[Kurt] is not simply a statement or storyline or supporting character used to build up the diversity of the gang. He is a person."

And here's the thing about Kurt: Television portrayals like his didn't predict a positive shift in attitudes toward gay people in America. They actually *contributed* to that shift. A study by the *Hollywood Reporter* found that 27 percent of the Americans who watched *Glee* or *Modern Family* (starring two gay dads) directly credited the shows with helping them become more pro–gay rights.

The more the nongay public was exposed to human stories about gay people—people with thoughts and feelings and families and desires and struggles like our own, the more empathy said public had for them. Oxytocin was part of the learning process that put us in Kurt's shoes. It helped make us care. Stories like these helped millions to decategorize gay people as a scary stereotype—an out-group—and see them as *just people*: part of our superordinate in-group.

Even though political issues like gay marriage remained charged, people who saw sympathetic stories of gay people became more willing to collaborate with them. By the time Titus Andromedon was stealing scenes in 2015's *The Unbreakable Kimmy Schmidt*, fewer than 19 percent of Americans said they were uncomfortable being around someone who is gay or lesbian. The fraction of Americans who thought being gay should be illegal went from half to a quarter. Ninety percent of the country said they would, for instance, feel equally comfortable with a gay salesperson. More than 70 percent said they'd be comfortable with a gay doctor, a gay presidential appointee, or a gay member of the armed forces. Fear and discrimination hadn't gone away, but openness had doubled in one generation.

Not that straight Americans have cause to pat themselves on the back. Of course the lion's share of credit for gay acceptance goes to brave everyday people (including a huge number in the entertainment industry, both behind and in front of the camera) who told the world they were gay even though they knew they would be persecuted. Surveys show that getting to know someone who is gay has a lot to do with changing people's attitudes.

And what do we really *do* when we get to know someone? We share stories. We relive the comedies and dramas of our past. We gab about what we're going through. In the restaurant. In the bar. In the break room. At the dinner table.

Unfortunately, there's a dark side to the power of stories. It has to do with the balance theory we learned about in the last chapter.

For much of the nineteenth and early twentieth centuries, the stories that went around about Asians in America had a huge effect on popular sentiment toward them. And not in a good way.

Books, radio, and early television portrayed Asians as either evil or witless. This gave schools and employers an excuse to deny them opportunities. The Japanese bombing Pearl Harbor was a true story made into a false pretense to incarcerate 120,000 Japanese Americans.

Note the absence of data in these decisions. Stories overrode logic. How often have you heard someone try to kill a statistic with an anecdote? "Well *I* read on the Internet there was this one guy who . . ."*

---

*On that note, it pains me to say that as this book was going through final edits in late 2017, a story came out in the *Hollywood Reporter* that a man had accused George of assault in 1981. George denied that this occurred, and the accuser later revealed that his accusation was exaggerated and no crime had occurred. However, much of the world will only remember that initial story.

This is classic balance theory at work:

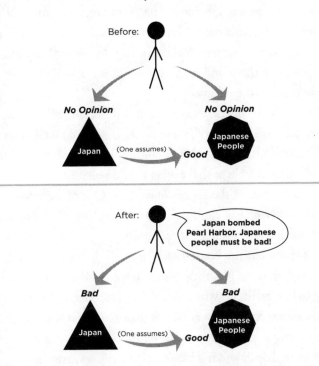

This is bad logic. Skewed balance turns a fearful story into mass guilt by association. Unfortunately, it's also effective. Because here's the crux:

Instead of turning on oxytocin, fearful stories give our brains an excuse to fire up our amygdalae.

One of the most devastating examples of this took place during the Vietnam War. US soldiers killed thousands of Vietnamese civilians after their leaders plied them with stories of how the Vietcong were evil. In 1971, Corporal John Geymann told the press that troops were taught, "It doesn't make any difference what you do to them; they're not human."

As historian Nick Turse, citing the mountain of documented evidence on Vietnam War crimes buried in the National Archives, put it, "The idea was that the Vietnamese, they weren't really people." From the moment soldiers entered basic training, he continued, "They were told, 'Never call them Vietnamese. Call them gooks or dinks, slopes, slants, rice-eaters.' Anything to take away their humanity, to dehumanize them and make it easy to see any Vietnamese—all Vietnamese—as the enemy."

This resulted in rapes, executions of children and elderly, and using civilians for target practice. This in turn led to brutal retaliations, and, in the end, thousands of soldiers coming home with post-traumatic stress disorder, unable to shake what they'd seen.

This is not new in the history of warfare. One of the most effective ways to rally people to do unspeakable things to other humans is to use stories that take away their humanity.

Isn't this what the Nation of Islam was doing in the early days, back when they taught that whites were devils? How could it be wrong to hate whites if whites aren't human? That Yacub story really did a number. X and others who left or reformed the sect later regretted using it to do something reminiscent of what racist whites had done in dehumanizing blacks with their own stories.*

Dehumanizing stories are an essential element of homophobia, too. Pundits have deployed anecdotes to support the argument that "gays aren't people," therefore gays aren't protected by the Constitution. Other dehumanizing stories include early horror films portraying monsters as thinly veiled metaphors for gayness, and absurd stories about predatory gay men turning straight men gay. These baseless anecdotes linger in folklore alongside vampires, kidney thieves, and the Loch Ness monster.

---

*The logic presented for why we were in Vietnam itself was especially dubious when compared with the war the government was simultaneously waging against black people leading up to the civil rights movement. If one were to quote Muhammad Ali, "I ain't got no quarrel with them Vietcong. No Vietcong ever called me nigger."

Stories have power. Stories can activate oxytocin and empathy, or they can turn on primal fear. Like fire, like steel, like nuclear energy, stories can be used for evil or for good.

On the "good" front, we find Lijiang Shen, PhD, at Penn State. In the late 2000s and early 2010s, Shen devised a cool set of science experiments wherein test subjects would sit down to watch public-service announcements about the dangers of cigarettes. While some watched ads centered on the familiar scare tactics—tracheotomies, amputations and the like—others watched ads designed to make them feel empathy for people affected by smoking. (Think things like brave children coping with lung damage from secondhand smoke.*) Shen found that both types of ads led some people to change their attitudes about smoking, but the fear-invoking ads had less of an effect. In fact, scary ads made many test subjects more resistant to changing their minds. Subjects reported that scare tactics put them on the defensive, making them feel as if their freedom to choose were under attack.

But empathy-inducing ads met no such resistance. These ads made people want to change on their own, no threat required.

Dr. Shen's findings have been corroborated by other research. Researchers in other fields have encountered the same phenomenon—among them CEO Robert Pérez, founder of the consulting group Wonder. In his work, Pérez has shown that people are more willing to do something scary—such as reverse a long-held belief about something they consider important—if they feel empathy toward the

---

*The National Cancer Institute estimates that approximately three thousand *nonsmokers* die each year from lung cancer caused by secondhand smoke.

person trying to persuade them. In one example, business owners who were afraid of hiring ex-convicts heard a presentation from another business owner in the same market. When their peer told them how hiring ex-cons could actually be an advantage, Pérez found that business owners were far more likely to change their minds than if they heard the same pitch from anyone else.*

Because stories are so good at inducing empathy, they help us become open even to people we *can't* relate to.

Imagine you're a manager, and you're having a hard time dealing with two bickering team members. They have different perspectives, and they aren't open to one another's ideas. Imagine you sit the two of them down together and announce that you're going to fire them both if they don't get along.

What outcome would you predict?

I think we'd both agree chances are good they'll take your threat seriously and stop openly fighting. But they won't *like* each other. You scared them into changing their behavior, but not their hearts. You've scared them into organizational silence.

Now imagine instead that you took these same two team members and told them they have to do dinner together. No talking shop—it's forbidden. They have to tell each other stories about their lives: where they grew up, how they met the most important people in their lives, their 10 Best, their blooper reel—that sort of thing.

Can you imagine them walking into work the next day having a little more empathy for each other? Treating each other a little bet-

---

*Perhaps this is why, similarly, research shows it's more effective for a stranger of our own race or gender to persuade us to stop doing things that are racist or sexist than it is for a stranger from our "out-group" to make the attempt. We have more built-in openness to people we perceive as in-group, therefore we're more amenable to their heartfelt plea that we get our shit together. Ironic.

ter? Even, dare I say, having each other's backs? Considering each other's ideas?

This is the power of stories.*

Jonathan McBride, the former assistant to President Obama in charge of staffing for the White House, has put this exact technique into practice at Blackrock, the world's largest asset manager, where he was a managing director at the time of this writing. Over several years, McBride and his associates developed a methodology for bringing different people together.

Blackrock had made a big push for cognitive diversity—and all the sorts of demographic diversity that should come with it—but over the years had run into the same things that we saw earlier with our failed mergers and team breakups. Different people can have a tough time getting along. If you're in the minority in a group, you're likely to get quiet. If your group has too much tension, the whole group can lapse into organizational silence. The upshot of a push like Blackrock's for more different team members was a lack of a feeling of "belonging."

McBride and his team did all sorts of little things to help reverse this, to help Blackrock employees feel like they could belong to a superordinate group, even though they might be different. This included training leaders to be conscious of opportunities for positive micro-actions, as Keith Yamashita taught us earlier. But the most powerful thing Blackrock did was teach people—employees and managers alike—to bond through sharing their personal stories with each other. These storytelling interventions, among other work, have led the company to become one of Fortune's Most Admired Companies, one of Human Rights Watch's Best Places to Work for

---

*And, sometimes, wine.

LGBT Rights, and one of LinkedIn's Top Companies "Where The World Wants To Work."

"You need people to care about each other," McBride says. "And how you get people to care is through emotional narrative."

7.

In late 2017, I flew to Los Angeles to visit Dr. Zak's neuro laboratory. There, on a Sunday morning, he strapped a device to me called an Immersion Sensor, which measures the downstream effects of oxytocin production in your brain. It does this by tracking changes in the vagus nerve, which is a big nerve that goes from your brain to your heart.

After strapping me up, Zak had me watch a video. It was a commercial for HP in which a father is trying to be a good dad to his teenage daughter. Throughout the video, he does nice things for her, and she ignores him or rolls her eyes like a typical moody teenager. At one point he takes a photo with her, which she's grouchy about. She later opens her lunch box at school to find this photo and a note from her dad. She quickly hides it.

Finally, the dad comes home after a long day of work, says hi to his daughter, who ignores him once more. He then walks sadly into her room. There, he looks around at all the signs that his little girl is growing up. He sighs and lies down on the bottom bunk of the bed she shares with her sibling and looks at the ceiling.

And on that ceiling he sees that his daughter has secretly saved all of photos that he'd taken with her over the years.

Are you tearing up? I was. Dr. Zak showed me the screen on which he was monitoring my oxytocin, and it showed very clearly where I started to experience empathy for this father. Throughout the video, I got little spikes of oxytocin as he tried to be a good dad, and at the end, I experienced an enormous surge of it.

I wasn't a father. I didn't know this guy in the video. I knew it was a fictional story. I had no reason to relate to his character. But after watching this little story, I *felt* for him. I liked the guy. I wanted to hug him.

This effect, Dr. Zak explained to me, "is melting that self-other divide." Positive social encounters release oxytocin—things like hugs, acts of kindness, and emotional stories. This oxytocin helps build relationships between people who are different, even people who are not inclined to accept each other. "If you release oxytocin naturally," Zak explains, "the in-group out-group bias disappears."*

I want to make sure you caught that. When our brains release oxytocin for a person who is not in our in-group, the bias we have for them *disappears*. And one of the key ways we can do that is through sharing good stories.

In the 1960s, the stories about Asian Americans went from scurrilous to approving. A lot of Americans developed greater empathy for their Asian neighbors—relating to them; respecting them, differences and all; allowing them opportunities long denied.

And this was partly thanks to Fumiko and Takekuma's son George.

---

*This may be a controversial statement to some scientists who don't know the groundbreaking research that was just published in the journal *Frontiers in Behavioral Neuroscience* by Elizabeth Terris, Laura Beavin, Jorge Barraza, Jeff Schloss, and Paul Zak: "Endogenuous Oxytocin Release Eliminates In-Group Bias in Monetary Transfers with Perspective-Taking." But it's true. And truly exciting.

8.

In 1966, television producer Gene Roddenberry made a phone call to a young Japanese American actor he had heard good things about. Roddenberry was working on a science fiction show that would feature a diverse case of problem-solving space adventurers. He wanted an Asian man to play the role of the spaceship pilot.

The show was called *Star Trek*. Its lead would be heartthrob William Shatner as the dashing Captain Kirk. Kirk's comrades: Leonard Nimoy as the wise Spock, DeForest Kelley as the sarcastic doctor "Bones" McCoy, and former jazz singer Nichelle Nichols as Communications Officer Uhura.

And in one of the first positive, de-stereotyped roles for an Asian American actor in Hollywood history, *Star Trek* would also star twenty-nine-year-old George Takei as the brave and clever Lieutenant Sulu.

Lieutenant Sulu didn't speak in a bogus accent. He didn't have insulting teeth, and he didn't blunder around crashing into things—the threadbare TV tropes of the day. Takei's character spoke precise English, with that rich bass of his, and masterfully piloted the USS *Enterprise*.

"As an Asian American, you always felt a real strong sense of excitement when you saw Asian people on TV," recalls Tony Award–winning actor B. D. Wong in a documentary about Takei's life. "And what's amazing to me now is how often those Asian people that you saw on TV were embarrassing."

But Sulu wasn't embarrassing. No yukata, no goatee, no sinister plotting. Sulu wore a Starship Command uniform and coolly collaborated with crew members. They trusted him with their lives. This was novel. And to B. D. Wong, this was an omen of change. "George," Wong recalled, "was this kind of beacon of dignity."

As *Star Trek* became a cultural phenomenon, George Takei's positive portrayal of Sulu reached millions. Takei was one of the first actors to tell a new story about Asian Americans. Thus, when a young athlete was discovered at a martial-arts exhibition in Long Beach in 1964, Bruce Lee was able to shatter the glass ceiling Takei had cracked. Pop-culture experts believe that Takei's pioneering role paved the way for Lee's international stardom.

New stereotypes were emerging. Hollywood was pushing the image of the Asian savant or the Asian action hero. Meanwhile, Chinatown—perhaps ironically—was pushing the image of the "upstanding Asian," working to supplant the old stereotype of the degenerate Asian in the press.

"The model minority myth as we see it today was mainly an unintended outcome of earlier attempts by Asians Americans to be accepted and recognized as human beings," said Dr. Ellen Wu of Indiana University. Wu's book *The Color of Success* documents Asian Americans' struggle for acceptance in the mid-twentieth century. "They wanted to be seen as American people who were worthy of respect and dignity. The Chinatown leaders were really smart. They started to peddle stories about Chinese traditional family values and Confucian ethics. They claimed that Chinese children always listened to their elders, were unquestioningly obedient, and never got into trouble because after school they would just go to Chinese school."

Smart? Yes. But people are people; kids are kids. Of course some Asian American children were obedient and some not; some Asian American families were close-knit and some not. The thing that actually changed between the time George Takei was imprisoned and the time George Takei was offered a part in *Star Trek* was the *story*. Asian Americans themselves remained fundamentally the same—good human beings deserving of inclusion and curiosity and respect. But the story being told *about* Asian Americans—at

the school board meeting, in the newspaper, on the silver screen—
was dramatically different in 1972 from what it had been in 1942.

You'll recall how Dr. Hilger's research concluded that Asian
Americans in the 1940s and '50s were simply held back by lack of
opportunities. As the stories about them changed, the opportunities
came. They seized them. This bred more good stories and more positive exposure to mainstream Americans, which in turn bred more
opportunities.

Discrimination is still alive and well in America, but Takei's and
others' stories helped to open people's hearts. More mainstream
Americans started letting Asians on the team.

9.

So who likes stats? (In my mind's eye I see every hand go up.
Hello, fellow nerds!) And who likes books? You, presumably—
since you've come this far.

Well, if you like books, you're going to *love* this next stat. As a
writer of books, I know *I* did.

In 2017, I took Dr. Krumrei-Mancuso and Dr. Rouse's assessment
for intellectual humility and added a few questions of my own.
Demographic information—where you've lived, where you've traveled, plus several other things. I asked thousands of people to take
this test, and as we discussed in the last chapter, I found a delightful
connection between living or traveling abroad and intellectual
humility.

One of the questions I asked involved traveling somewhere a
little less expensive: into books.

Take a look at what the survey data show us when you compare
intellectual humility scores with how much people read books:

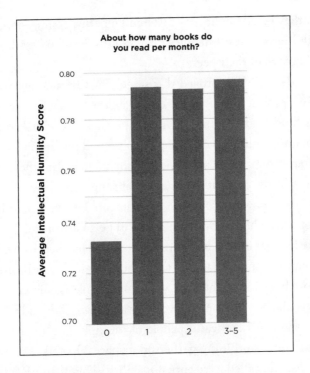

People who read a book or more per month, the data shows, are significantly more likely to be have IH than those who rarely read!*

Reading lots of books means we're taking in lots of stories about lots of people and things. Is it really a quantum leap to suggest that doing so will give us a little more openness toward the people we meet in everyday life?

In 2010, a professor named Dr. Delia Baskerville of Victoria University put this theory to the test when she brought a bunch of young students from different cultural backgrounds together for story time. She found that when kids participated in story time together—sharing stories about themselves, their cultures, and other

---

*Hopefully this means the demand for authors like me won't go away . . . !

things they cared about—it "fostered empathy, compassion, tolerance and respect for difference." These kids grew to be a little less xenophobic than their peers.

In 2014, Dr. Zak proved this same effect from a neuroscience angle in a project for DARPA. Zak's lab, the Center for Neuroeconomics Studies at Claremont University, once again hooked people up to brain-chemical-tracking devices. It found that inspiring stories across out-groups made people less xenophobic toward those groups and more likely to donate to causes that supported them.

The most powerful of these experiments involved an animated video of a little black boy who wanted to be an astronaut. The adult real-life brother of this boy narrated how his brother, Ronald McNair, once had a librarian call the police on him when he asked to check out books from the library. The police told the librarian to let him have the books. Ronald loved to watch *Star Trek*, and while his brother thought the idea of people of multiple races—including a black person—working together on a spaceship was pure science fiction, Ronald called it "science possibility." Eventually, Ronald became a physicist, and the second African American astronaut in history. Tragically, he died aboard the *Challenger* shuttle in 1986. And the library that once tried to deny him books renamed itself after him.

People in Zak's lab who watched this animation showed all the signs of empathy, generated oxytocin, shared heartfelt comments about the story, and donated a lot of money to an African American–related charity when asked afterward—regardless of their own race.

"Narrative transportation was the strongest predictor of charitable behavior," the Center wrote, referring to viewers' reports of being "pulled in" by such a good story, "followed by the experience of empathic concern." Race didn't matter when people saw the story. Ronald McNair was a human being, and part of their team.

It is melting that self-other divide. If you release oxytocin naturally, the in-group out-group bias disappears.

My research shows how books can be a great way to experience stories and open our hearts this way. Gallup and Pew research about gay rights attitudes shows us how stories on the screen help us do this, too. The New Zealand study and the positive results at Blackrock show how stories from one person to another help us feel like part of the same team.* Dr. Zak's DARPA study showed us how watching a *cartoon* about a black kid's dream of going to space, and his subsequent death aboard the *Challenger* space shuttle after becoming a groundbreaking physicist made people of all races feel more connected to, and empathy for, black people.

Knowing this, we shouldn't be at all surprised by what happened when George Takei and other Japanese Americans shared their story with Washington.

In 1983 the congressional Commission on Wartime Relocation and Internment of Civilians (CWRIC) formally admitted the grave injustice the United States had done by interning Japanese Americans. Since 1980 the CWRIC had been holding public hearings around

---

*I think one of the key benefits of a liberal arts education is the exposure of stories through art, literature, theater, film, and music as a way to cultivate our imagination and empathy for the way others experience and interpret the world. This doesn't require a college education or any sort of formal educational setting, but I do think it is enhanced in discussion with other people. Sharing our own experience of any of these arts forms with other people forces us to articulate what we think and feel, and it puts us in the position of hearing what others think and feel. The variety of ways in which we can cultivate our individual imaginations and capacity for empathy is staggering, and it all points back to sharing stories. The more we engage in the arts, the more we will increase the worldwide talent pool for Dream Teams.

the country, learning the experiences of Japanese Americans* whose lives were upended during the war. More than 750 people testified, among them George Takei, who spoke at hearings held in Los Angeles in August of 1981.

George told the commission about being forced into that camp. He told them about playing inside the barbed wire fences, in the shadow of the machine guns. He shared how his parents' hopes and plans and hard-earned home-ownership goals had been crushed for no better reason than the way they looked.

Takei's story stirred empathy with the public, and it resonated with members of Congress. The CWRIC report was instrumental in President Reagan's decision to sign the Civil Liberties Act of 1988, which included a small, mostly symbolic monetary apology to survivors of the camps. Nineteen forty-two was a long time ago, but these stories still made people care. And they made a difference.

But internment wasn't the only way George Takei had been confined by prejudice. For the first sixty-eight years of his life, Takei never spoke on the record about being gay, though it had been an increasingly open secret among fans since the '70s. George had made a name for himself in Hollywood at a time when a California law allowing involuntary sterilization of homosexual people was still on the books. For decades George had lived with the tension between who he was and who the public wanted him to be.

But when then-governor Arnold Schwarzenegger vetoed a California same-sex marriage bill in 2005, George Takei felt he had to take a stand. After formally coming out in an issue of *Frontiers* magazine, Takei launched Equality Trek: a speaking tour that brought his story to college campuses around the United States. Takei had

---

*The commission also heard testimony from Native Alaskans forcibly relocated from the strategically important Pribilof Islands in the Aleutian archipelago.

long been active in California politics and LGBT organizations, but with Equality Trek, George was taking his story nationwide.

And can you guess what happened?

To thousands of fans, George the actor became George the person. George Takei helped college kids and Trekkies alike see the gay rights movement for what it is: a quest for the equal protection of ordinary people under the law. As social media grew, Takei used his fame, his story, and his sense of humor to build a gigantic Facebook following.

More than a decade after formally coming out, George Takei was still sharing stories to build support for social justice. In 2013, he was declared the Most Influential Person on Facebook, having touched tens of millions of people through sharing stories—both funny and heartfelt—about human beings deserving of the world's empathy and respect. At the time of this writing, Takei was screening a Broadway musical he created, called *Allegiance*, about the Japanese internment camps he grew up in. It was just another way to use stories to teach about how locking Japanese Americans up in 1941 and discriminating against gay couples in 2017 are just different symptoms of the same disease: excluding people because of who they are.

Winning respect for Asian Americans was not a solo project. Nor was winning gay rights. By sharing his story, and playing a part in the stories of *Star Trek* and others, Takei helped recruit collaborators in both efforts. He helped build the gigantic Dream Team of people that every social movement needs to make progress.

If storytelling could do all that, imagine what sharing our stories can do at smaller scales. Imagine how stories might help humanize those with whom we have tension—in our partnerships, our companies, our coalitions. Our causes. Our families. Imagine what stories might do for our teams, when we haven't developed the respect and intellectual humility to properly harness our differences together.

Imagine how those stories might help us learn to love the people we fear instead of shutting them down.

10.

In 1967, as *Star Trek* began its second season of filming, George Takei arrived one morning to his dressing room to a surprise.

Inside the room were two costumes. While Takei had been filming a side project, the screenwriters had written in another character to work as ship's co-commander. Walter Koenig, playing the character Pavel Chekov, would now be sharing the helm with Takei.

Takei was furious. "I'll admit it—I hated him," he recalled. He was jealous that someone else would be splitting the role he had worked hard to develop. "The veins in my scalp started to swell up."

When Koenig showed up to the dressing room, the first words out of his own mouth were, "I hate this!"

"Well, I don't like it any better!" Takei retorted.

Koenig hesitated. "You do, too?"

"Of course," Takei said. "I don't like it any better than you do."

"Well, at least you don't have to wear it," Koenig said.

Takei then realized that Koenig had not been talking about having to work together. He was talking about the floppy wig in his hands that the producers were making him wear.

Embarrassed, Takei set aside his temper for a moment and let Koenig talk. As he listened to the man's story, Takei's heart began to soften.

He learned that Koenig had also attended UCLA, that he had a brother who worked in medicine, that he had been working long and hard for an acting break so his family would respect his career choice. "I saw that he was an ambitious actor excited by the opportunity of being part of a quality television series, just like me," Takei said. "The hate that had tempered down to pity, then tolerance, was now softening to a recognition of our matching lives and shared ambitions."

After learning Koenig's story, Takei couldn't help but swallow his pride and work with the man. "We were in this together," he said.

So they teamed up. They leaned on each other. They commanded the starship *Enterprise* together. And the image of Sulu and Chekov sharing its console became one of the iconic images of not only *Star Trek*, but of the kaleidoscopic Dream Team that humankind could one day become in Earth's actual future.

And forty years later when George Takei married his sweetheart, Brad, in Los Angeles, Walter Koenig was his best man.

EPILOGUE

I want to end this book by telling you about the worst day of my life.

You wouldn't think it was the worst day by the way it started. That's what's so ironic:

My day started at the new SoHo offices of my growing company, which after three years of one-hundred-hour workweeks had become a real business—and had at that point created more than fifty jobs. I'd started it with two friends and a stack of credit cards. We'd poured everything into it, this dream that was finally coming true.

After a good day's work, I left my friends at the office and hustled uptown to interview a famous billionaire onstage in front of one thousand people at Columbia University. We'd be talking about the launch of his latest book, and a little bit about my first, which I'd published a week before, fulfilling a fantasy I'd had since I was in middle school.

At the time, it was the largest crowd I'd ever spoken in front of.

Afterward, I quickly shook hands with everyone and ran out the door. I grabbed the 1 train downtown to Soho House, a fancy social club where people richer and cooler than me hobnobbed and drank wine. A group called the Influencers had invited me to speak about my work to an intimate gathering of smart and famous people—musicians and entrepreneurs and heads of advertising and modeling agencies. The crowd included one of my childhood heroes, Bill Nye the Science Guy.

My speech was a hit. I was on fire.

After the presentation, Bill Nye shook my hand and congratulated me on my work. World-champion beatboxer Rahzel stopped me on my way out and said he couldn't wait to read my book.

It was just after one in the morning by the time I got out of there, with a pocket full of business cards. I walked out the Soho House doors onto the cobblestone streets of the Meatpacking District.

And then I remembered that I had no place to sleep that night. You see, I was homeless.

While on the outside I was at this great inflection point in my career, on the inside I was suffering from the worst series of emotional setbacks I'd ever faced. It had started with a cancer scare and ended in a surprise divorce request—everything at once. Subsequent hasty negotiations had left me broke, depressed, homeless, and wondering whether any of this work stuff even mattered.

Only a few people in my life had much idea what was going on with me behind the scenes. I hadn't even mustered the courage to tell my family. Much less my employees. I was co-running a business worth millions but secretly unable to afford a deposit on an apartment.

Rather than asking a friend to let me crash for the three months I'd need to save up for a rent deposit on an apartment, I'd been bouncing from couch to couch, keeping details light and feeding off the generosity of pals and acquaintances and trying not to "burden" any one friend unduly.

This was obviously a dumb plan.

But, having been a bastion of stability and sobriety for twenty-nine years, I was now spiraling out of control in both senses. I was too anxious to talk with people about my situation and wouldn't allow myself to stay with anyone for too long, for fear that I would have to fess up to having passed out on a park bench or the L train a few too many times. Or to talk about how I was feeling.

And in the frenzy of this day's speeches and events—a day that should have been one of my greatest—I had once again forgotten to arrange somewhere to stay.

I pulled out my phone.

It had only 1 percent battery power left.

I frantically texted my friend Nat to ask if I could crash. The phone died.

And then, as if the universe were filming some sort of tragic movie, the clouds above New York began spilling their guts.

I slumped down onto the curb. Sitting there in the rain on the corner of Ninth Avenue and Fourteenth Street with the backpack that contained my entire life in it, I broke down.

I had never felt this alone.

All the years of work I'd put in, all the hours and weeks and months and sacrifices to get to this day that should have been so happy. Everyone in that auditorium thought I was such a success. Everyone at Soho House assumed I had everything going for me.

I couldn't feel more opposite.

After a few minutes and more than a few deep breaths, I fumbled around my bag for the keys to my office and started a rainy, two-mile trudge.

Anyone who is lucky enough to be alive has a lot to be grateful for. I knew that, for a variety of reasons, I had it better than a whole lot of people out there. But that didn't make me feel better. I didn't know whether I wanted to put one foot in front of the other anymore—or not.

You're holding this book in your hands because a group of people helped me find my footing again.

The first was a man named David Carr.

He was a columnist for the *New York Times* who, after writing about my company a year before, had become a friend. He'd call me occasionally to talk about stories he was working on, or for help with some tech-related thing for the new college class he was teaching.

Shortly after that night at Soho house, I was tromping around New York with my backpack, killing time, ruminating about the point of it all. My cell phone rang. It was the raspy voice of Mr. David Carr.

He launched into whatever it was he had on his mind. But after a moment, he stopped.

Something was wrong. *What was it?* he asked.

David was good at getting people to cough up information. I cracked. I unloaded all the gory details. I told David everything.

He listened, said a few curse words on my behalf, and told me about the times that he—a former crack addict with a divorce and a few jail stints under his belt—hit rock bottom himself.

And then he told me the words that no one else would tell me.

"It's going to hurt. And that's okay."

For whatever reason, that acknowledgment was a wave of relief. Avoiding the pain was only prolonging it. And besides, if he'd been through things like this and become the world-famous writer and happy family man that he now was, I didn't have to worry that I could pull myself up, too.*

The second member of Team "Resuscitate Shane" was my apprentice, Erin. She had signed on for a few months to help run things at my company while in between a couple of her own ventures. Little did I know when I hired her, she was also a spiritual giant with a heart of gold.

As people at work started to hear rumors about what was going on, I got lots of, "Are you all right?" and "It's going to be all right."

---

*Devastatingly—and for many, many more people than just me—David passed away a couple of months after this. But he kept checking in on me up until then. I got a tattoo in his memory. I'll never forget him.

Erin, on the other hand, forced me to stop and do breathing exercises. She made me go to yoga class. She gave me pep talks. She got all Buddhist on me. And she said what I actually needed to hear.

I listened to what she said. And I got through it.

It's not easy to admit to yourself that you can't solve all your problems yourself. But doing so helped me move forward during that dark time—and every dark period since—instead of staying stuck on my own suboptimal mountain peak, mired in my own fear.

The real lesson that I learned during that brief and devastating period of my life is not about any particular coping mechanism for grief or self-pity. It's that the best way to make progress when the going gets tough is with each other. David and Erin—and all the rest who helped pull me out of the abyss: my partners Joe and Dave, my dear friends Lazer and Jess and Simon and Frank and Kosta and Maria (and even you, Jon Levy!)—were the combination of wonderful and disparate people that I needed to break through and move forward. They were my Dream Team.

The most important things are made easier—made possible—together. Sometimes those things are as small as changing the world. Sometimes they're as big as changing a life.

SPECIAL AFTERWORD

⌐⊕¬

with Sheryl Sandberg and Adam Grant
(and a few illustrators from around the world)

Sheryl and Adam are two of my favorite modern examples of Dream Team builders. As COO of Facebook, Sheryl has built one of the most impactful teams in business history. She is also the author of *Lean In* and creator of the Lean In Together movement for workplace equality. Adam is a professor of organizational behavior at Wharton and has pioneered groundbreaking research on collaboration as author of *Give and Take* and *Originals*. Together Sheryl and Adam are the coauthors of *Option B*, a masterpiece that has helped me and thousands of others to get through hard times together, and a wonderful *New York Times* series on Leaning In together.

As a little treat for the end of *Dream Teams*, we put together the following Q&A for an inside look at their process and philosophy on collaboration that I think can help us all get a little better at working together without falling apart:

———⊖⊖———

In what ways, beneath the surface, are you two different? And how do those differences help (and/or stall) your collaboration?

As writers, we gravitate toward different styles. Sheryl's writing is infused with vivid imagery. "Lean in." "Sit at the table." "Kick the elephant out of the room." Adam is more abstract; he explores what it means to be a "giver" or "taker," a "procrastinator" or "pre-crastinator." She prefers the magnifying glass; he likes the telescope.

We have different ways of writing our first drafts. Kurt Vonnegut wrote about the distinction between swoopers and bashers. Adam is a swooper: he writes "quickly, higgledy-piggledy, crinkum-crankum, any which way." Sheryl is a basher: she writes "one sentence at a time, getting it exactly right" before going on to the next sentence.

We also have different taste. Sheryl loves structure and organiza-tion. She wants every idea to flow logically to the next one, every point to have a practical application. Adam is more inclined to let a story meander and then introduce a reveal—an unexpected twist.

We've found these differences invaluable. When we write to-gether, we find that we generate bolder ideas and more vibrant im-agery than we would alone. And we get a better mix of speed and quality, structure, and surprise.

———⊖⊖———

On the surface, you two are a somewhat unlikely pair of collaborators. How did this team-up come about? And what keeps the caper going?

In March 2013, Sheryl published her first book, *Lean In*. A few weeks later, Adam published his first book, *Give and Take*.

That summer, at a conference, Adam ran into Sheryl's husband, Dave Goldberg. Dave invited Adam over for dinner. Adam will never forget walking into Dave and Sheryl's house. Their daughter, who was five at the time, asked him how his day was. Then their son, just seven years old, told Adam that his "daddy had taught him about the book" and started asking questions about it.

After dinner, Sheryl started asking Adam about gender differences in his data. (Sheryl remembers this as a series of questions. Adam remembers this as a "grilling.") The next day, on a cross-country flight, Adam reanalyzed a decade of his data with Sheryl's gender-related questions in mind, and he was horrified by what he found. It was just as Sheryl had written in *Lean In*: men got more credit than women for helping others. And men were rewarded for speaking up with new ideas and suggestions, while women who did the same were either barely heard or judged as too aggressive.

Adam told Sheryl what he found, and they decided to write a series of op-eds together on women and work. They discovered that they both love evidence, and that Sheryl's leadership expertise and Adam's research complemented each other.

Writing collaborations tend to go in one of two directions. Either you become real friends or you decide you'd rather not see each other for a very, very long time. We're glad our collaboration went down the first path.

Divergent views can lead to a deeper Understanding

#dreamteams

— Sheryl Sandberg & Adam Grant

Toby Kistanov

There's a tension between the reality that group work is often frustrating and the truth that we can't accomplish really big things on our own. In your work, what have you seen make the difference between a group that breaks down and the group that breaks through?

The late Richard Hackman spent his whole career studying groups that work and those that don't—from symphony orchestras to airline cockpit crews and intelligence units to basketball teams. He identified five key conditions that enable teams to succeed:

- A real team: there's a core group of people working on a task that truly requires collaboration.
- A compelling direction: there's a clear vision and a motivating goal.
- An enabling structure: roles are clearly designed and defined to leverage each person's strengths.
- A supportive context: the team has the rewards, education, information, and reward they need.
- Expert coaching: knowledgeable outsiders are available to teach, motivate, and consult as relevant.

"Together...we generate bolder ideas and more vibrant imagery than we would alone."
–Sheryl Sandberg & Adam Grant

————————⬡————————

In your work together, was there a perspective or opinion or finding that forced one or the other of you to reconsider your own strong viewpoint? What happened?

When we wrote our *New York Times* series together, we knew we wanted one article to be about gender differences in helping others. It's a topic we both find fascinating, it was where our first books converged, and we had new data to report. Sheryl wanted to lead with the idea that we take helping for granted when it comes from women (she's communal, she wants to help) but we celebrate helping by men ("I never expected him to think of others, I must now shower him with praise and rewards"). Adam was concerned this theme wasn't novel enough, since it had been a prominent point in *Lean In*. Sheryl made a persuasive case that you don't have to say something new if you say something that's true. We went with it, and she was right. "Madam C.E.O., Get Me a Coffee" might be our most popular article together.

————————⬡————————

We each
have
something
to learn
from
each other.

–Sheryl Sandberg
& Adam Grant

#dreamteams

Fabiola Correas

———⊕———

What are the ingredients that matter for people to be able to fully "lean in together" to work for equality when those people are very different—or see some things very differently?

The most critical ingredient for any collaboration, but especially between people who are very different, is mutual respect. You have to believe that you have something to learn from each other—and when you disagree, instead of assuming that the other person is wrong, it's far better to recognize that divergent views can lead to a deeper understanding of the problem and a novel set of possible solutions. That's about making the most respectful interpretation of someone's point of view. Of all the ways you could explain someone else's words, start with the one that presumes good intentions, not bad intentions.

———⊕———

———————⊕———————

What do we need to do in order to simultaneously achieve equality and leverage our uniqueness in order to make progress together?

Many people want to fit in and stand out. These can be competing motives, but we often pursue them in tandem by searching for what psychologists call "optimal distinctiveness": a sense that we're the same and different at the same time.

The easiest way to get there is to create unique groups, which give us the simultaneous feelings of belongingness (I'm part of a group) and uniqueness (this group is different from other groups).

When women join Lean In Circles to support each other's ambitions and champion equality, they often create "optimal distinctiveness" by highlighting something that stands out about their particular Circle. In the military, there's a Combat Boots and High Heels Circle. In Northern California, there's a Millennial Latinas Circle.

Anytime we come together in a group, when we emphasize what's unique about our mission—or something rare that we share in common—it helps strengthen our bonds.

———————⊕———————

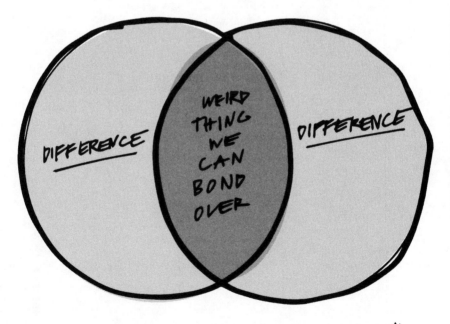

"Emphasize what's unique about our mission—or something rare that we share in common. It helps strengthen our bonds."

— SHERYL SANDBERG + ADAM GRANT

DIFFERENCE

WEIRD THING WE CAN BOND OVER

DIFFERENCE

— JESS BLACK

———⊕———

Who is your favorite superteam in history?

Sheryl: Tina Fey and Amy Poehler.

Adam: It's a toss-up between Jerry Seinfeld and Larry David, Marie and Pierre Curie, Lincoln's team of rivals, and Jerry Siegel and Joe Shuster.

(Shane: Adam, that's like four teams!)

———⊕———

"The most critical ingredient for collaboration, especially between people who are very different, is mutual respect."

→ Sheryl Sandberg & Adam Grant

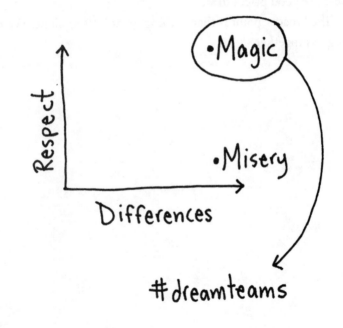

#dreamteams

J. HAGY

---⊗---

The world has a lot of problems today that will require a lot of different people to come together and collaborate to solve tomorrow. What can we do to help bring people together to fight our problems instead of each other?

Sheryl's foundation has created two kinds of communities to do exactly this: Lean In Circles and Option B groups. If you care about gender equality or helping build resilience in yourself or others—and we believe these are two critical issues facing our world today—these are good places to start.

The broader point is that nothing great is done alone. We make progress together.

---⊗---

DREAM TEAMS CHEAT SHEET

———⊕———

A few simple strategies to make better teams.
Dig in deeper at: shanesnow.com/dreamteams/strategies.

TEAM FORMATION:

❑ Recruit for "culture add" not "culture fit."
❑ Recruit for ability to elevate team, rather than for individual stats.
❑ Determine team members' dimensions of internal and external differences and life experiences that could lead to different Perspectives, Heuristics, and "How You Roll."
❑ Make sure everyone on the team knows each other's "superpowers" or unique abilities.
❑ Take a two-step approach to problem solving.
    ❑ Define the problem as Novel vs. Not, High Stakes vs. Low Stakes.
    ❑ "Cast" the group that should be working on this problem together, based on the type of problem (the more novel and high stakes, the more important team member differences will be).

INCLUSION:

❑ Accumulate micro-opportunities to include people and have them mix with each other.

❑ Whenever a group will be affected by a decision, make sure someone from that group is "cast" as part of the team, regardless of seniority level in the group.

❑ Ensure that everyone in a problem-solving process gets equal opportunity to participate.

❑ Give team members flexibility to do things their own way, in exchange for accountability.

STAYING IN THE ZONE:

❑ Use play and humor to depressurize group tension.

❑ Give explicit permission (or even rewards) to dissent, critique, and blow the whistle.

❑ Have team members get to know each other's stories—especially when in conflict.

❑ Debate instead of brainstorm; when necessary, switch sides of the debate.

❑ Speak candidly, un-anonymously, and without holding back.

❑ It's the leader's job to make sure tension does not get personal.

EXPANDING THE POSSIBILITIES:

❑ Seek diverse sources of information, not just team members.

❑ Develop and prioritize curiosity.

❑ Pay attention to outsiders, weirdos, and far-out ideas; suspend your reflex to ignore them.

GETTING UNIFIED:

❑ When possible, rally teams around superordinate goals; when not possible, emphasize the meaning of the challenges you want the team to come together to solve.

❑ Celebrate the uniqueness of the subgroups within the big group.

❑ Allow group members to have their own values; don't push yours on them. The only values I recommend in all cases are Inclusion, Speaking Up, Curiosity, Respect, and Intellectual Humility.

❑ Create unique rituals that the superordinate group can do together to bond like a family, ensuring that they don't potentially exclude anyone or step on anyone's personal values.

BECOMING OPEN:

❑ If you can afford it, spend significant time immersing yourself in places with cultures different from your own.

❑ Get a multicultural education: learn a language, watch TV in another language with subtitles, get to know different kinds of people and food, explore the arts with curiosity

❑ Take in a variety of books, movies, and television.

❑ Build bridges by sharing personal, emotional narratives.

SPECIAL FEATURES

⊙⊙

So, this was fun, but what next?
If you're hungry for more, check out the following:

Bonus / Secret Chapters:
shanesnow.com/dreamteams/bonus

Research Notes & Bibliography:
shanesnow.com/dreamteams/endnotes

The Making of Dream Teams:
shanesnow.com/dreamteams/behindthescenes

Assessments & Exercises
shanesnow.com/dreamteams/superpowers (cognitive diversity)
shanesnow.com/dreamteams/ih (intellectual humility)
shanesnow.com/dreamteams/om (open-mindedness)

And get Shane's newsletter for exclusive updates, articles,
and more adventures at **shanesnow.com/report.**

SPECIAL FEATURES

JOIN THE TEAM

Liked *Dream Teams*? Here's some things you can do!

Write a review for others to see what this is about:
shanesnow.com/dreamteams/review

Tell your teammates:
shanesnow.com/dreamteams/share

Give a copy to a friend:
shanesnow.com/dreamteams

INDEX